ANGEL
Relationships

A MATCH MADE IN HEAVEN

Annette Bruchu

REDFeather

MIND | BODY | SPIRIT

Cover design by Danielle Farmer

Type set in Minion/Great Vibes

ISBN: 978-0-7643-5509-7

Printed in China

Published by Red Feather Mind, Body, Spirit
An imprint of Schiffer Publishing, Ltd.
4880 Lower Valley Road | Atglen, PA 19310
Phone: (610) 593-1777; Fax: (610) 593-2002
E-mail: Info@schifferbooks.com
Web: www.redfeatherpub.com

For our complete selection of fine books on this and related subjects, please visit our website at www.schifferbooks.com. You may also write for a free catalog.

Schiffer Publishing's titles are available at special discounts for bulk purchases for sales promotions or premiums. Special editions, including personalized covers, corporate imprints, and excerpts, can be created in large quantities for special needs. For more information, contact the publisher.

We are always looking for people to write books on new and related subjects. If you have an idea for a book, please contact us at proposals@schifferbooks.com.

In loving memory,
I dedicate this book to my daughter,

Leah

who is with the angels.

I also dedicate this book to my children and
grandchildren with the wish that they may begin to
better understand their own relationships
with their angels and guides.

Contents

Acknowledgments

Angel Relationships: A Match Made in Heaven is brought to you with the help of so many angel messages from beyond.

I would like to thank my angels that understand me better than I understand myself. Their many messages infuse me with a sense of wonder, and keep me on a fulfilling journey, in a way that can only be meant to be.

Thank you to my wonderful editor and brilliant ghostwriter, Natalie Fowler. Her knowledge of the material and expertise has been priceless.

Thank you to an incredible woman, Lorri Rice. I have shared with you dreams that are strange, and dreams that woke me in the arms of the angels. Thank you for your support, encouragement, and everything you've done to help me along my path.

I give gratitude to all of my many friends and family for their expertise, advice, and enthusiasm.

I am grateful for the encouragement I have received from thousands of people whom I have talked with about their belief in the angels and their loved ones among the angels on the other side.

I couldn't complete this project without special thanks to Jim Bruchu, my loving husband. I also have a special thank you to Neil and Billy Bruchu for their loving support and wholehearted hugs along the way.

Foreword

Angel energy is all around us, all of the time. God created the angels and instructed them to devote their heavenly energy and higher intelligence to us mortal humans. God created the angels for a specific purpose, so that we would not have to walk alone on our life's path. Our angels walk with us, every single step of the way. Because they come from God, and have a direct connection to God, they know us better than we know our own selves, and their love for us is unconditional. They are filled with pure love, and they use this love to guide, encourage, and inspire us to use the best qualities of our soul, in other words, our gifts.

Because the angels are divinely devoted to us, miracles are possible every single day. I wrote this book so that others may pause and take notice of this celestial daily intervention. These pages offer assistance to awaken the spiritual window in your mind's eye, so that you may hear, see, feel, and know that angels are present in our lives. Believe in them, trust them, love them, and be grateful, for they are there for you.

Using the angels, explore the healing aspects of your own aura and energy field. Connect with them to receive knowledge and guidance. Find tools to help make the connection with your angels even stronger. Understand how the angels are speaking to you. Learn how to better fit the angels into your life every day. Then, go forth and fulfill your passion and purpose in this life.

When I was working on this book, sometimes, I would get my words directly from the angels themselves. During the editing process, every now and then we recognized these angelic voices rising up, loud and clear. In an effort to preserve the divine message from the angels themselves, we preserved these messages intact, sprinkling them throughout the book.

This is just such a message, a promise from the angels, to you:

An Angel Message

I promise I will stay connected to you, with hope you
will understand my guidance and direction. Just hold my hand
and believe in me. All will be all right.

Ways to Use this Book

The topics covered here grow gradually. Each topic includes visualization exercises or meditation ideas designed to help you get to know the angels in your life. This book contains lots of activities, specifically designed to be something you can *do* to help grow your connection with the angels.

This book can be read cover to cover, and by the end, you will have a solid understanding of the many ways angels are present in our lives. And your connection with the angels will be stronger for it.

It can also speak to you in times of trouble. Simply pick it up, set an intention for what you need to find within its pages, and the angels will help you find the right page when you flip it open. You may also find a favorite section that resonates with you, and maybe you will return to those pages again and again. In short, use it however these pages (I mean, the angels) speak to you.

At the end of the book, I have also included special angel messages and thoughts for each day of the week, each month of the year, each season, and also some special life events.

No matter who you are, and what you believe in, anyone and everyone can connect and be present with their angels.

PART ONE

Our Angel Connection

THE BASICS
What, and Who, Are the Angels?

Angels are superior beings; they are the messengers between God (the divine) and us (the mortals.) They serve both us and God, offering themselves as a bridge between.

Angels assist us with their guidance for the purpose of helping the greater good. When we put forth good intentions, we enable the angels to act divinely on our behalf. Sometimes, the outcomes are delightfully unexpected. Although the results may be unexpected, we can always know that the element of certainty throughout is that the angels were involved.

Angels have distinct personalities. They love to connect with you in your dreams, sing when you are singing, and laugh out loud with your joy. Angels love to feel good, and their connection with you is at its strongest when we show our true personality and express our real self and feelings.

Boost this connection by consciously choosing the colors you wear each day. Do you feel enlightened? Wear lavender. Do you feel lovable? Wear rose. The colors you wear provide and attract the energy you will need to get through your day.

COLOR	MEANING
Yellow	Playful; Joyful; Nurturing; High levels of communication
Green	Practical; Open to learning
Blue	Holds spiritual space; Calmness
Violet	Visionary; Sensitive
Red	Passionate; Driven
Pink	Loving; Spiritual; Caring; Sensual; Tender
Blue	Deep feelings; Communication; Peace; Love
White	Spiritually motivated; Transcendent

Here on Earth, we have the gift of free will and make choices all day long. Our choices not only affect the outcome of our day, they can affect our future. From their vantage point on the heavenly plane, angels have a view of the big picture and a larger, broader perspective. It's as if you were playing a game of chess, looking down at a chessboard. But instead of having to make all of the moves by yourself, sitting behind you is an expert chess strategist. This expert is always available to help you walk through the various options and understand the different outcomes. Angels wait patiently for us to make our choices. And yet, if we ask them for help and guidance, they can give it. By learning how to listen to our angels, we have access to expert strategists that can guide us through our life game.

The next time you are faced with a choice, consider asking your angels for guidance. Imagine yourself playing a game of chess. The different possible choices in your dilemma represent your next possible moves in the game. Instead of picking up your piece and moving it right away, consult your strategy expert. Ask your angel (out loud or in your head) to show you the possible moves and help you see the different outcomes. Have a pen and note pad ready to take notes if necessary.

There are a lot of different angels, ready to jump in and help us. But first, it is important to know and understand the role of our Guardian Angels.

Guardian Angels are sometimes referred to as Everyday Angels or even Birth Angels. Joining us at birth, these angels are available every single day to help us stay on task, and they can help us see the world from a different perspective. With wisdom and without struggle, they stay close, always. They become our best friends, delivering messages and bringing us signs of moving forward. They borrow ideas for us to use, lead us to do what's right, and warn us when danger is lurking.

Imagine yourself at a party. Everyone is wearing those blue and white name tags that say, "Hello, my name is _____." The very next person you turn to meet, happens to be your Guardian Angel. What does their name tag say? What do they look like? Imagine yourself having a conversation. Ask them about their job as your designated angel. Ask them to share their most favorite moment in your life thus far. Ask them about the most frustrating parts of their job. Maybe, thank them for sticking with you through those frustrating parts and ask them to tell you more about what they do for you. Are they serious when they speak? Or maybe they have a sense of humor?

When Guardian or Birth Angels join us as we are born into this world, they do so with a promise to never leave our side throughout the duration of our journey through life. No matter how harsh the journey may become, they make a promise to stay with us through both the good and the bad. By their very nature, you are the center of your Guardian Angel's existence.

Close your eyes. Imagine that your angel takes you by the hand. Imagine your angel speaking these words to you: *I promise, that no matter how harsh your life journey becomes, I will be here with you. I will try to raise your spirits when you are sad, and I will hold your hand when you get lost. I will be your voice when you can't speak, your ears when you can't hear, and your eyes when you can't see. I will help you to set your course and be your internal compass to direct you through life. I am grateful that we are in this together.*

And know that your angel has been whispering these words to you, over and over since the day you were born.

Your Guardian Angel is your built-in best friend. Your best friend is there to comfort you when you feel alone. Be reassured that your every thought and all of your words are heard.

The next time you feel alone in this world, close your eyes and imagine that you are going for a walk. Maybe it's down a city street or maybe you follow a path through the forest. As you walk, imagine that your Guardian Angel joins you, and maybe even takes your hand. Feel a wave of comfort wash over you. Feel that presence next to you, and know from a deep, internal place of knowing, that your Guardian Angel is always with you, walking by your side.

Our angels know us better than we know ourselves. They know each and every thought that we have, even when there are as many as hundreds per minute. Some of our thoughts even come to us directly from our angels. Your angel can communicate with you through passing thoughts and sometimes, as an inner knowing. If we learn to recognize these thoughts and this inner knowing, we won't accidentally ignore our angels.

An Angel Message
At just the right time, I will intervene within your thoughts.
For I am your Angel, a Celestial Being, so light and so pure.
I will deliver my message for your interpretation.

Reflect on a time when a thought popped into your head and you wondered where it came from. Think of a question you want to ask your angel. Notice. Does a thought randomly answer the question? If it doesn't happen right away, keep trying. We are working to build the connection and trust that it will. When a random thought does answer a question you ask, know and trust that it is your angel, speaking to you from within your thoughts.

Our angels look forward to the moments when we show an interest in them, or attempt to communicate with them. It is almost as if our angels come alive when we remember that they are there walking beside us. We can never ask too much from them. Because they are from pure love energy, their job as angels is never overwhelming to them.

The next time you are outside on a sunny day, pay attention to your shadow. Notice how it is always walking by you, waiting for you to move, and then it, too, moves right along with you. The more you move, the more your shadow moves. Our angels are always with us, just like our shadows. When we talk to them, ask assistance from them, and show gratitude for them, we free them to be animated and involved in our lives. But always remember, we don't need a sunny day. Our angels are there for us whenever we ask, and most especially when it gets dark.

We are on this Earth plane to connect and socialize with others. Sometimes, we pick up the phone to chat, other times we text or email. Sometimes, we even make plans to spend time together and have conversations in person. Our angels exist on a different, universal plane. We need to connect with them by crossing from our earthly realm to their Angelic Realm. But it's easier than it sounds; we were born with the right communication tools, and we can activate this conversation any time of the day or night. By speaking words out loud, thinking words in our heads, and also through our emotions and expressions, we can activate this angel hotline.

Think about the ways you reach out to your best friend. Do you prefer to talk on the phone or send a quick text? Now, think about all of the different ways you can reach out to your Guardian Angel. When you cry, you call them to your side. You can speak words out loud and they are there to listen. Or you can think thoughts in your head, and they will answer.

An Angel Message

Our connection is special and unique; it only connects between you and me. I can hear your cries and feel your tears. I am there with you through all of those painful experiences.

This connection with our personal angels is private. It is just for each one of us, individually. It is as if we have been given a special password. This password holds a code within it, and this code states that our angels will never fail us.

Imagine yourself looking up at the most beautiful, brilliant, stained glass window you've ever seen. Now, a cloud clears, and a beam of sunlight spills through it. You are lost in the beauty of the color, and the sight fills you with warmth. The echoes and chatter of others falls away, leaving you captivated by the moment. Every time we connect with our angel, it's like that.

Our Guardian Angels do not judge. Always and in everything, they only want what is best for us without judgment or condemnation. We live this life with free will and choice. Because we are having a human experience, we are not perfect. We will make mistakes. Our angels never judge us for these mistakes, and they understand that we are here on Earth walking in this lifetime to learn certain lessons. They only want us to learn these lessons so, ultimately, we become better in and for this world.

Think about a time you made a mistake. It could be a big mistake or a little mistake. Perhaps it was one that left you filled with regret. Imagine your Guardian Angel, standing there in front of you. Your angel reaches out and wraps their arms around you. Patting you on the back, your angel doesn't scold or chastise you, they simply say, "I understand. Let's move forward in a different direction."

Our connection with our Guardian Angel is a journey in our hearts and mind. It is the journey of a lifetime and the connection is based on pure, unconditional love. This love connection began before we were even born. Our Guardian Angels were matched to us and selected for us by a higher power and we can go through our life journey knowing the best possible match was made.

Never forget that your Guardian Angel *gets* you. They know you from before you were born. They know what kind of child you were growing up. They know every mistake you've ever made and every triumph you've ever overcome. If you are known for your sense of humor, joke with them. If you have a serious nature, be serious. The more you are yourself with your Guardian Angel, the stronger their connection is with you.

Each one of us is unique. We have each had different experiences in life that combine to make our own personal treasure maps. Angel energies dwell in us, around us and through us. Angels will align us with the right friendships and relationships to help us succeed along the way.

Think about the important people in your life and the different roles they have served. Some may have been confidants; others may have been your personal heroes. Still others may have played the role of a villain or maybe even your nemesis. All of these people were brought into your life and crossed your path to teach you a lesson of some sort. Each and every one of them helped you get to a different spot on your life's treasure map. Know that your angels helped arrange every single one of these relationships.

Now that you know and are aware of this, go forward in life, observing and taking notice of who comes in and out of your life, and considering what purpose they might have or lesson they bring.

Your inner most thoughts can be soft, quiet, and tender. Your soul is receiving that whisper as a message that passes through your mind. This inner dialogue is a conversation between you and your Guardian Angel. Whispering thoughts are all that you need to connect. Listen to the soft intuitive whisper, for it brings guidance. This whisper guidance is pure and white, and is intended to make your journey lighter.

 Listen to the whispers. As you go through your day and interact with various people, friends and family, coworkers and store clerks, notice how people talk to each other. How do different people communicate with each other? Notice that the more familiar the relationship, the closer and quieter the conversation may be. For example, an exchange between a cashier and customer, is efficient and polite but not at all intimate. However, a mother who comforts her child after he falls at the park, will be quiet, tender, and loving. A mother's care and concern is filled with love and comfort. Know that this is how your angels will always talk to you. Sometimes, you have to quiet the noise of other voices around you in order to listen and hear.

Finding this connection with our Guardian Angels changes our life journey. A doorway into new beginnings has been opened. An end to old thought patterns of worry and fear is in sight. Our angels have been waiting for this moment. Celebrate your arrival at this doorway to enlightenment.

 Imagine yourself staring at a wall. It is so long that you can't see the end of it in either direction. For awhile, you've been walking along it, trying to find a way around or through. And then, you reach a doorway. Your hand twists the knob and the door opens, allowing you passage to the other side. All of your frustration and worry about finding a way around or through the wall melts away. Greeting you warmly on the other side is your Guardian Angel. Your angel is excited to see you, and has been waiting for this moment for a long time. Your angel can't wait to show you all of the opportunities on this side of the wall.

As we allow ourselves to open up to the new opportunities that are presented when we embrace the angel presence in our lives, sometimes, our emotions become stronger, and our space may need to be balanced and cleared. There are various ways to balance and clear space, and these will be discussed. For now, it is enough to set a simple boundary.

 Imagine yourself in a protective bubble. Only allow light and love within it, everything else bounces off the outside. Ask your angel to guard your bubble, and keep it intact.

An Angel Message

With every turn you take, and every road you travel,
I will follow you and fill you with memorable moments. Take notice of
the majestic beauty that surrounds you, your simple observation will
help us connect. At just the right time, as your angel, a celestial being so
light and pure, I will intervene within your thoughts to be with you
and to deliver messages for your interpretation.

THE TIME IS NOW

Now is the time to embrace our angels' presence in our lives. Now is the time to live without fear. Trust that there is a spiritual connection, and keep it constant. Do the work to strengthen this connection so that it does not get lost or grow stagnant.

Say these three simple words out loud: "I am ready."

The angels want us to understand that, with them, we can be a step ahead of whatever situation is at hand. Angels can reroute a situation and cause delays, allowing us to avoid trouble. They can also align connections and get rid of overwhelming setbacks.

The next time you find yourself thinking, "Wow. That could have been me," stop and say thank you to your angels. Because it could very easily have been a situation where they intervened on your behalf to make sure it wasn't you.

An Angel Message

It is my job to pay attention to your thoughts and desires.
I hear them all and want to help you in any way I can.

STAY IN THE MOMENT

The light of our Guardian Angels is in front of us and behind us. It is meant to help hold us together. If we try to live too far in front of this light we might find ourselves too worried about the future. If we try to live too far behind this light, we might be caught up in the past. When we live in the now and stay grounded in the present moment, we are perfectly aligned with this angel light. When we live in the moment, our hearts are able to find the greatest peace, and this is where the connection to our angels is the strongest.

Find a symbol of the now. It could be a simple token you carry in your wallet, a scrap of ribbon you tuck in your pocket, or a necklace or medallion you wear around your neck. When you touch it or see it, let it be a reminder to you to stay in the present moment.

An Angel Message

Chat with me; tell me what is on your mind.
I want to bring you experiences of joy and top that off with more joy.
It might be in ways that are a mystery for you. As your angel, I will send
you a nudge, or maybe a whisper, a personal message, just for you.
We can speak in silent thoughts.

BUILDING YOUR ANGEL ENERGY

A current of infinite energy flows in us, around us, and through us, always. All living things have a vibrating frequency of energy. For some, this current of energy is amplified and intense. Anything living can give off energy. Electromagnetic energy can move through our body with ease; it can move through our palms and fingertips and also through our thoughts.

The elements provide energy, too. For example, wind, water, fire, and air all give us energy to utilize. The Earth itself stores energy. Mountains, rocks, and stones carry megahertz (MHz) that can reflect energy to each of us individually.

The next time you are outside or go for a walk, look for an ordinary stone. Try to find one that is no bigger than your thumb. Pick it up. Hold it. Know that it is no ordinary stone at all. This stone holds earthly energy. Hold it and tune yourself into its energy to truly feel the current it holds within it. It holds the vibration of laughter from the land. It holds memories of stories untold, and it is a gift from Mother Nature, just for you. Allow the spirit of this simple stone to guide you naturally, to protect you, or naturally connect you to your inner spirit. This stone is now a symbol and holds divine guidance.

The next time you have a choice to make and you find yourself in a moment of indecision, try this. Close your eyes and imagine the different choices spread out in front of you—except, they are off in the distance, and you can't quite see what they are. Now, imagine that you are holding this very same stone. You have tuned into its energy; it holds divine guidance just for you. Use your imagination to throw your stone. Follow after it. Where does it land? Which choice does it make?

MIND'S EYE

Fortunately, we have a built-in tool to see this energy, commonly known as our Mind's Eye.

Closing our physical eyes, we can look through our closed eyelids. When our physical eyes are relaxed, our minds will adjust and open and expand to the world of more awareness.

Close your eyes. What do you see behind your eyelids when your eyes are closed? Colors? Objects? Energy? Pay attention to this energy and the colors that appear. Take notice of more and more detail coming into focus. Ask questions in your thoughts to your Guardian Angel to help you identify the images you are seeing. Do the pictures and shapes you are seeing come with a feeling in your gut?

Sitting comfortably, take notice of an object in the distance. Hold a focus on that object. Now, relax your eyes and gaze into the softness around the object until it begins to appear as a 3-D image. See it morph and change as you relax. Now, close your eyes and slowly open them once again. Does the space between you and the object begin to show you different images? This magical, inbetween space will begin to bring forth messages from your Guardian Angel.

Next, try looking at a living object, like a plant or person. How is it different? As you learn to relax your sight and exercise this new muscle in your brain, you begin to hone the skill of going deeper into the world of energy.

OPENING YOUR THIRD EYE

Your third eye is a thought center located in the area of the pineal gland in the frontal lobe of the brain, between your eyebrows. Your third eye is like a room with a view to the past, present, and visions of the future. It has no limits. To strengthen this muscle in your mind, use it regularly.

When you are in a relaxed state of mind, perhaps when you are going to sleep at night or waking up in the morning, practice going into this room. Without expectation or intention, simply look around. What do you see with your third eye?

Through our third eye, we can also connect our spirit's energy with our angel's spirit energy, and in doing so, we can connect to the universe of wisdom and truth. This will bring us internal vision and knowing. Through our third eye, our Guardian Angel can lend us ideas and help us increase our awareness. The purest form of this awareness is our trust and faith in our Guardian Angel.

Imagine a white cord of energy, extending from your third eye. Imagine it to be somewhat like an umbilical cord. It reaches up and connects to your Guardian Angel in the Angelic Realm. Through it, your body is able to fill with white, angelic light. Step back for a minute, and see yourself and your connection to your angel.

Our senses serve as the perfect measuring tools. They are perfected, just for us, to breathe in air and to smell if something is fishy. We use our five senses (sight, hearing, feeling, tasting, and smell) all day, every day. We can see, hear, smell, and feel rain. We can taste a cup of coffee and feel the mug grow hot in our hands.

Look around and observe what you can see with your eyes. Close your eyes and listen. What do you hear? Close your eyes and reach out your hands. What do you feel? Notice your level of certainty. When you take a sip of coffee, you know it's coffee. When we close our eyes and hear a dog bark, we know it's a dog. We trust the information we receive. We are confident our answers are correct. This is the level of certainty we will try to attain as we develop our supernatural, psychic senses.

The bottoms of our feet are really sensitive to touch. Take off your shoes and socks to walk barefoot on the floors, carpet, concrete, or on a sandy beach. Tuning into this sensation will heighten this sense within your body. With each and every step, this sense slightly raises the entire body to feel more sensitive. The body's cells are awakened and you become conscious of each and every step you are taking. The more observant and sensitive you become, the easier it will be to connect with your angels. Use this exercise whenever you feel it necessary to tune your own body into your physical senses. By walking barefoot and feeling all that is under your feet, you become more aware of your thoughts and learn to pay attention to different details.

We are all filled with energy. We also have built in barometers and sensory apparatus to pick up and read energy around us. These are psychic gifts. In some people, some of these built in tools are stronger than in others, but we all have them and we all have the ability to further develop them. Within some of us, certain tools or psychic gifts may be stronger than others. But where one gift might be stronger than another, we can still work to develop all of the different psychic sensory apparatus.

Our psychic senses, or extrasensory perception, provides tools and helps us communicate with our angels. Sometimes, people have these psychic gifts without even understanding or knowing that they have them.

Think about the different ways you might be reading or receiving different energies. Do you sometimes hear words in your head? Answers to questions you've asked? Maybe when you close your eyes, you see images of people, events, or symbols. Maybe, when you tune yourself in, you get a feeling of certainty, one way or another, about different situations. Or maybe you are good at helping your friends solve problems by just "knowing" what they should do. Perhaps you smell different smells, like cigar smoke or an apple pie baking in the oven, when there is no earthly reason or explanation for this smell. And finally, perhaps you get a taste in your mouth for no apparent reason.

CLAIRVOYANCE

A clairvoyant receives intuitive information visually.

Sometimes clairvoyants have a gift where they can "see" energies with their own eyes. This could be aura colors surrounding a person or maybe even spirits or ghosts standing there in front of them. But clairvoyance also includes the images we see with our third eye when we close our eyes. Do you get pictures that pop into your head? That is clairvoyance.

Close your eyes. What do you "see" when your eyes are closed?

CLAIRAUDIENCE

Clairaudience is the ability to receive intuitive information through hearing.

Sometimes those with the gift of clairaudience hear voices that belong to others. However, sometimes, when your mind is settled and you "hear" thoughts, maybe you "hear" them in your own voice. This is still clairaudience. Even if it's your own voice whispering answers or words of wisdom, it is still psychic information coming in.

Close your eyes and settle your mind. What do you "hear" when everything else is quiet?

Especially listen to the thoughts that interrupt your routine. These are important messages from our angels.

The next time there appears to be a random thought interrupting you during a daily routine task, stop and write it down. Note the details of what is happening around you; they may be important to the message you are receiving.

Can you hear the ringing in your ears? Our angels operate at a different frequency and vibration than we do. Thoughts travel like lightening waves around us. Angels love this telepathic depth of communication.

Ask your Guardian Angel to help you tune your frequency to theirs. Imagine them, tuning a dial on the radio until they come to the channel that is yours. Then ask them to "turn it up!" and also imagine them turning up the dial for the volume.

We can harness the powers of telepathy to send others good thoughts as well. Telepathy is the transmission of information from one to another without using any of the five senses. When we are in sync with another person, the body can send and receive messages through the energy grid to the receptors in another. Bees communicate through a similar dance of energy. So do our Guardian Angels.

Play with telepathy. The next time you are somewhere with other people, send someone a hello through a thought. Maybe you are sitting on a bus, or maybe you are at work. Do they turn their head to look at you? What is their reaction to the thought you sent? Different people have different levels of telepathic ability. Have fun observing who responds and who doesn't.

CLAIRCOGNIZANCE

Claircognizance is an inner knowing. The ability to know something, without any substantiating fact. Our Guardian Angels can connect with us via feelings.

Think about a time where you just knew something was right. You couldn't explain how you knew, you just knew. Perhaps it was confirmed by a feeling in the pit of your stomach. This is claircognizance.

CLAIRALIENCE

Clairalience is the ability to obtain psychic information through the sense of smell, in other words, smelling something that isn't there. This is one of the most rare of the psychic gifts.

Our sophisticated smell sensory apparatus can be in tune to thoughts, feelings, and memories. Certain smells connect to the receptors in the brain that are related to the receptors of how to react or behave. When we trust our sense of smell, our teams of angels can utilize this sensory ability and signal us to pay closer attention in a situation. It can be a reminder, or even a warning.

Think about your favorite, or most memorable smells and what they mean to you. Perhaps it is the smell of your favorite dinner, simmering on the stove, or maybe your grandmother's apple pie. Or maybe, your grandfather was a smoker and he always had solid advice about life for you. By cataloguing certain smells with an identified meaning, your angels can use these as signals to you. For example, when you smell your grandmother's apple pie, it can be a sign of comfort, sent by the angels. Or if you smell your grandfather's cigarette smoke, it can be a signal to remember and heed some of his advice.

CLAIRGUSTANCE

Clairgustance is the ability to receive psychic information through taste—in other words, tasting something that isn't really there.

Have you ever had a bad taste in your mouth for no apparent reason? The next time you get a bad taste in your mouth, consider that your Guardian Angel might be warning you of something and take note about what it might be.

CLAIRSENTIENCE

Clairsentience is the ability to feel the emotions of others around you. Clairsentience is the gift of inner feeling. People with the gift of clairsentience are also called empaths. This is one of the most common psychic gifts. It can also be one of the more troublesome.

Close your eyes and tune into your own emotions. How are you feeling? Happy? Sad? Do these emotions correlate to your personal experiences of the day?

We are all emotional beings, living in an emotional world. Empathetic people are common. In fact, a lot of empaths are walking around on this Earth and have no idea they are empathetic. Empaths feel the energy and emotions of others, sometimes very strongly.

Empaths have a higher degree of knowing when something is wrong. It is very easy for them to understand the truth with clarity. Empaths can respond quickly if someone is troubled, sick, or not telling the truth. But an empath doesn't always recognize that sometimes they are picking up on the energy and emotions of others. Sometimes, they feel this energy and emotion as their own, without knowing or understanding that it came from someone else. This can cause nervousness and upset to their own systems.

An Angel Message for Empaths

Your energy is sensitive.
You have a heart that is filled with compassionate expression.
While this will make it easier to connect emotionally with your angels,
you may need training and assistance to better understand your gifts
and learn to recognize which emotions are yours,
and when you are reading the emotions of others.
Whether it is through laughter or tears, it is your responsibility
to understand how and why you feel what you feel.

 The next time you are called to comfort someone who is upset—perhaps it is a coworker who is upset about a decision, or maybe a child is afraid, or a friend wants to complain about an injustice—pay attention. Tune into the different emotions of the situation. Take note of the upsetting emotions. Are the upsetting emotions becoming your own? Practice sympathizing and empathizing with the upset person, *without* taking on their emotions for yourself.

With each new generation, we grow and evolve mentally and physically. But each generation can also have different energetic and psychic traits. In recent years, there has been such a shift and significant increase in the numbers of highly sensitive and psychic children born into this world, that they have been given unique descriptive categories. These children are often referred to as Star, Indigo, Crystal, and Rainbow children, and each category has different psychic and energetic qualities. The result, though, is that we sometimes find ourselves not understanding the generations that came before us, nor do we always understand the different generations that come after us.

 Think back to your grandparents. Did you ever hear them say something like, "Kids these days!" Words like these were also usually accompanied with a shake of a head and a stern look that only a grandparent filled with age and wisdom could manage. Have you ever found yourself wondering about the younger generations? Maybe questioning why they think or act a certain way? Let these memories or observations help you understand that there really are innate differences between different generations.

An Angel Message

The answers are within you, trust in those thoughts.
Trust your senses.

COLLECTIVE ENERGY

Once we begin to understand the energy of living things around us and how it works with our own energy, we can begin to understand the collective energy.

The thoughts, prayers, and intentions of everyone, everywhere, are sent out to the ethers of the universe. These energies align and combine with the energies within the Angelic Realm. This network of energy waves braids together in a special and unique way. This braided energy allows and provides for transformation and miracles. It truly makes anything possible.

The next time you say a prayer or set an intention, imagine it as a ribbon of energy leaving you. It flutters out into the ether and eventually reaches up into the Angelic Realm where the angels reside. There, it finds your Guardian Angel. Your angel takes the ribbon and very carefully weaves it into the collective braided energy of every intention, everywhere. Through this braid, your intention aligns with the intentions of others, making it possible for miracles to happen.

Collective energy, with devotion and practice, can build and become stronger. It is ours and can be there for us to grasp onto during times of turbulence or transformation. Hold onto it, for it will tether you to the angels, and you will know that you are never alone, and anything is possible.

The next time you find yourself in a frustrating situation, picture this braided cord of energy connecting you, strong and firm, to the Angel Realm. Reach up, grab this braided cord of energy, and give a tug, just like you are ringing a church bell. The more frustrating the situation, the harder you should grasp the rope, even use two hands if you have to. Pull. And know that by pulling tight on this cord, you've called your very own angel to your side.

MERKABA ENERGY

Merkaba energy is divine energy. It can be seen through a sacred geometric structure. Every time it spins, the lights interlock, creating a vortex of divine light, moving at the speed of breath. By creating Merkaba energy, we can raise our energy and connect our light body to the higher, divine realms of the angels. Creating Merkaba energy is as easy as being aware of our breath. By being aware of our breath, we are activating a connection to the higher realms.

Sit in silence. Set an intention to extend your personal energy to flow in a direction that is an extension of you. Take a deep breath in. As you breathe in, visualize a circular force moving clockwise that begins with your energetic field and extends beyond. With each breath, this energy grows and expands, until it reaches as far as you want it to go, all the way up to the realm of the angels. By setting the intention to extend our own energy, we create Markaba energy that can reach and connect to the divine Angelic Realm.

Breathe in a rhythm. From your core, take a deep breath, and as you exhale, imagine a ribbon of energy spinning up your spine. Take as many deep breaths as you need, to get the energy from the base, all the way up to the top of your head. When you are finished, change your breathing to more shallow breathes. As you take each shallow breath, imagine the energy flowing up your spine in a continuous, gentle, circular pattern.

We will talk more about pendulums a little bit later, but here is an exercise you can do with a pendulum to "see" Merkabah energy and access its healing power. Hold your pendulum between your thumb and forefinger. Allow the chain that is holding the pendulum to swing ever so gently from the palm of your hand for a few minutes. Notice its pattern. This activates the chakra in the palm of your hand and allows it to open and flow.

We can send energy up to the heavens and the Angelic Realm, but as we walk forward in life, we also leave a ribbon of energy trailing behind us. This helps others to follow and find their way as well. This flowing ribbon of energy is not just a connective link to our Guardian Angels; it allows our gifts and talents to combine with our passions and purpose. Your ribbon is your energy, and it can change color and shape. Your ribbon flutters through your aura field and, with awareness, can be used to move results forward. The effect can bring happiness through a more empowered way of life. We can be even brighter when we consciously direct our ribbons.

Think about the rhythmic gymnasts that dance and move with the long ribbons. If they were to simply walk forward, holding the ribbon stick, the ribbon would drag on the ground. However, their goal and purpose is to never let that ribbon touch the ground during their routine. They flip, twist, wave, spin, and jerk that ribbon, and the result is a beautiful dance. Be careful not to let your own ribbon drag on the ground.

AURAS

Our energy fields extend to assist the connection with our angels. Our auras have many different layers, and are an extension of us. These energetic layers affect us personally, emotionally, spiritually, and cosmically. The layers consist of a fluid vibrational flow of molecules and emanate our experiences and beliefs. They have a color frequency and simulate sound waves and a color wheel, combined.

The light of the aura energy around us is the most beautiful of the energy fields. Each person has their own unique aura print. Aura colors reflect personality characteristics, strengths, and weaknesses. This is the color of your life, filled with all of the love that you give and receive. Aura colors can be bright or pale. Our aura fields also house our beliefs, sometimes self-limiting ones, and our emotions. When we care about what color it is, it makes it easier for our Guardian Angels to find us, see us, and be there for us.

The different aura colors are:

COLOR	MEANING
Yellow	Intelligence and humor
Orange	Creativity and originality
Violet	Sensitivity and visionary
Blue	Spirituality and understanding
Red	Force of will and passion
Green	Practical and analytical

Spend some time thinking about your own aura. What color do you think your aura is? What color do you want your aura to be?

Our auras emanate more than light and color; they also give off a vibration that can be felt in the Angelic Realm. When our Guardian Angels are looking down at our auras from the perspective of the Angelic Realm above, it is like watching an amazing Fourth of July display of "sparkle-icious" color in the sky.

Consider having your aura energy read, or even have an aura photo taken of yourself. Knowing our aura colors helps us understand our own strengths and weaknesses.

The next time you have the chance to sit in a crowd of people—maybe at the airport waiting for a plane, or on the bus, or even at a park—take a minute to sit on a park bench, and watch people walk by. Stare at something off in the distance to relax your eyes. When your eyes are relaxed, scan the different people walking around you. It is especially helpful to look out of the corner of your eye. Can you see anyone's aura colors?

Imagine that you are sitting with your angel, up above, maybe on a cloud. Look down at the earth and tune into the aura colors of everyone moving about below. Watch the colors move and explode, almost as if you were watching a fireworks display, but in reverse. Know that we are each our own version of a firework, special and unique. Our colors explode when we live our authentic self, follow our passions, and share our light and love with the world.

Polishing our auras is important. Keeping our auras polished keeps our vibration clear. Guilt, disarray, chaos, and mayhem are all things that cloud our auras. One way to polish our aura energy is to fill it with laughter, love, and joy.

The next time you find yourself laughing at something funny, think about your aura colors. Imagine them getting bright and shiny as your laughter grows.

The next time you go outside on a fresh, crisp day, think about the air flow swirling around you; imagine that the air goes in, through and around your aura and energy field. As it does, imagine that the air is "polishing" your energy field and colors. Imagine your aura colors getting brighter and bolder.

The next time you take a shower or bath, or even go for a swim, imagine that the water is rinsing through your aura field, cleansing the colors and energy field. If you like to soak in a bath, Epsom salt, sea salt, and minerals can also facilitate a cleanse of your aura energy fields.

CHAKRAS

The chakra system runs along our spine and, within our energy layers, holds our emotional centers. Our basic chakra system is always operating, even without us consciously acknowledging it. There are seven primary chakra centers, each one is a different color.

1. The root chakra is red and located at the base of our spine and is the emotional center for survival skills.
2. The orange sacral chakra center is just above the root chakra, and it is the emotional center for creativity.
3. Our yellow solar plexus is the emotional center for confidence and intuition. This is where our "gut feelings" come from. It is located in the abdomen.
4. Our green heart chakra is the emotional center for giving and receiving. It is located in the chest.

5. Our blue throat chakra is the emotional center for communication.
6. Our brow chakra is violet and houses our third-eye and is the receiver for our extrasensory perception.
7. Our crown chakra is white and is located at the top of our head. It is where divine ideas and inspiration flow in, connecting us to our higher-self and our higher power.

When the chakra systems are running smoothly, in balance and harmony, the energy wheels associated with each primary center are synchronized and spinning together.

Sometimes, when we feel pain in our bodies in any of the above areas, and nothing physical is wrong or can be diagnosed, more than likely there is an imbalance or even a blockage to one of our chakra systems. Sometimes, a chakra system can be overextended, and one of the energy wheels is spinning faster than the others. Problems with an overextended chakra system manifest in different ways. Our chakras can also underperform in which the energy wheel is spinning slower than the rest. Professional energy workers can help balance our chakra systems to achieve better health. But there is a lot we can do by ourselves to help keep our chakra systems running smoothly.

Our angel work becomes easier and more effective if our chakra energy fields are balanced. There are a lot of ways to balance our chakras. Energy healing, massage, meditation, and even exercise are all different methods to balance our chakras and can help put us in a calm state of mind. This balance will then carry us to a higher sense of perception. It can be even more effective when we set out with an intention in mind. This intention is important because it creates a structure between ourselves and our angels and that in turn helps to build trust between ourselves and our angels.

Energy healers are becoming more accessible and are easy to find. There are many different modalities for practicing energy workers. Reiki and healing touch are just a couple of the different methods. Consider looking for an energy healer who you could use on a regular basis. As we open up our psychic energies and expand our own energetic capabilities, it is good to have someone who can help keep our energy fields healthy and working smoothly.

If you are someone who likes to get a massage, the next time you have one, before you begin, take a quiet moment alone to ask your angels to help use this massage to balance and reset your chakras.

Are you someone who likes to work out to chill out? Maybe you are a runner or a swimmer, or like to go for long walks or hikes with the dog. Maybe you like to play hockey or soccer. Whatever your preferred method of exercise, the next time you set out for your walk or go to play a sport, pause for a moment to set your intention. Whisper something like the following to yourself: "May this activity help me to balance my mental and emotional state, and make me feel better about myself and my world."

Yoga is a great way to clear your chakras. The disciplined movement shifts our bodies and chakras into place. Holding a pose builds strength and invokes calm. Yoga classes uniquely blend empowerment while at the same time nurture our souls. The open heart pose is especially good, it embraces the chakra of the heart and reminds us that true love begins within.

Likewise, being out in nature, no matter the season, can also serve to ground our energy and naturally clear our chakras. When you find yourself feeling unsettled, go outside. Breathe in the fresh air, feel the rain on your skin, or even lay down on the grass. Let nature and the Earth balance out your energy and help reset your chakras.

By combining intention with visualization and imagery, we can quickly and effectively synchronize our chakras to work together. I like to call them, "chakra-sizes." Choose the one that resonates with you, and use it often. Or, mix them up and try different exercises each time. Feel free to adapt these exercises as necessary. After trying some of these, you and your Guardian Angel, might even come up with your own visualization that is customized and tailored just for you.

When you get in the habit of clearing your chakras, you will be able to recognize and know when there is an imbalance, before it becomes a problem. When you are in the practice of meditating and working with your chakras, you will also be able to fix an imbalance very quickly.

It is easy to balance your chakras for yourself during a meditation. Simply visualize the seven spinning wheels of light. You can picture these inside your body, or outside going up along the back of your spine. The first is red, at the base of your spine. The next is orange, just above the red. Next is yellow at your gut or belly button, then green at your heart. Blue is at your throat, then purple at your brow. On top of your head, is a white spinning light. Next, visualize a steady stream of white light connecting from the top of your head, up to the heavens.

Another visualization is to imagine that the back of your spine is a beautiful, silver flute. Each of the chakra centers is a different note on your flute. Take a deep breath in and watch as your breath enters the top hole of the flute, gently traveling through the flute as you fill it full. Then, exhale, ever so slowly and gently. As you exhale, imagine each of the different notes, playing in harmony.

Play with the chakra colors. Change and adapt your visualization to what works best for you. You can take each color in turn, and imagine different colors of flowers, swirling around you. Or maybe you have a sweet tooth. Imagine different colored candies swirling around you. Our angels like it when we get creative. This is a great visualization to adapt for children. You don't need to explain to a child what each of the different colors mean, but you can easily talk them through a chakra clearing exercise at night.

Maybe you have children or grandchildren of your own, or maybe you get to babysit for a favorite niece or nephew . . . the next time you are with a child, consider practicing a chakra exercise together. These will work best at bedtime or before a nap. When the child is tucked into bed and the lights are out, have them lay calmly and quietly and take a few deep breaths to settle their energy. Next, introduce different colors in the order of the chakras, one at a time. First, have them think of a red flower, or even red sparkly stars. Have the stars (or flowers) swirl slowly around their body. Next, introduce the orange stars, then yellow, then green, then blue, violet, and white . . . until all of the stars are swirling together around their space. Tell them the stars will help them heal any cuts or bruises they have, and help them have good dreams all night long.

The Root Chakra

The root chakra, located at the base of our spine, is the emotional center for survival skills. When the root chakra is overextended, it can manifest itself as an overactive libido. Someone suffering from an underactive root chakra might come across as a professional worrier. Their sense of safety and security is rocked by the smallest of threats.

To balance the root chakra, take off your shoes and walk barefoot. Make your steps even and controlled. Next, add a bit of a stomp to your step. As you stomp, imagine the spinning red wheel of your root chakra jiggling back and forth with each step. Each strong step brings it more and more into balance.

The Sacral Chakra

The orange sacral chakra is the emotional center for creativity. An overextended sacral chakra can manifest itself as someone with a lot of really great ideas, but an inability to see them to completion. An underactive sacral chakra can simply show up as a lack of creativity.

To balance your sacral chakra, do pelvic exercises. Lay on your back with your hands resting at your side, palms on the ground. Slide your feet up so that the bottoms of your feet are flat on the floor and your knees are up towards the ceiling. Pressing through your feet, and supporting yourself with your hands, raise your hips into the air. Rock your hips back and forth, up and down. Imagine the orange spinning wheel, or your sacral chakra, balancing itself into place.

The Solar Plexus Chakra

The yellow solar plexus chakra is the emotional center for confidence and intuition. An overextended solar plexus chakra can manifest itself in a large and inflated ego. An underactive solar plexus chakra can reveal itself through insecurities and feelings of inadequacy.

 To balance your solar plexus chakra, find a hula hoop and give it a spin. The rocking motion will rock the spinning yellow light of your solar plexus chakra back into place.

 If the hula hoop isn't your thing, find some music and dance. The best music for this exercise is an "oldies" station. Find music that makes you want to twist your core back and forth, and "do the twist." As you twist and move, feel your center chakra find its balance and even itself out.

The Heart Chakra

The green heart chakra is the emotional center for giving and receiving. The heart chakra is specifically designed to feel love and compassion for others through acts of kindness and appreciation from others. The passionate energy of love flowing from the heart chakra can even travel through our hearts and down through our arms and out our hands and we can give it to others through touch. Someone with an overextended heart chakra simply gives too much away. Worn out and exhausted, they end up with nothing left for themselves. An underactive heart chakra manifests itself in qualities of being demanding and selfish. A person with an underactive heart chakra takes more than they give.

 To balance your heart chakra, sit with your legs crisscrossed in front of you. (Crisscross, applesauce.) Stretch your arms straight out to the side, holding your palms away from your body. Take three deep breaths, and imagine the air flowing through all of the chakra centers. Now, take one arm, and wrap it around the opposite side of your body, under your arm pit. Take your other arm, and tuck it over your opposite shoulder. Notice that you are giving yourself a hug. Hold this position for another three breaths. Squeeze your arms a little tighter each time. Feel yourself, squeezing your heart chakra into place. The breathing motions help it to grow and expand as necessary. Repeat until you feel like your heart chakra has been balanced. Next, do a few pushups. The pushups will activate your newly balanced heart chakra to synchronize itself with the rest of your chakra centers.

The Throat Chakra

The blue throat chakra is the emotional center for communication. Have you ever heard the expression, "They talk a mile a minute?" Someone with an overextended throat chakra speaks at a fast rate, often saying more than 2,000 words per minute. An underactive throat chakra can manifest itself as someone who is too quiet and non-communicative. An imbalance in our throat chakra can also reveal itself in chronic sore throats.

To balance your throat chakra, gargle with sea salt water. As you rinse your mouth and go through the motions of gargling, imagine the water, swirling around and polishing your throat chakra so it looks shiny and new.

Singing also helps to balance our throat chakra. Turn on your favorite song and sing along. Or better yet, sing without any accompaniment at all. It can be a song you make up, or a song you know and love. If you need to, build into it. Start out by humming a tune. Hum the notes until you hear them in tune. Then gradually build into words. Sing until every note sounds like it is in tune, crystal and clear.

The Brow Chakra

The violet brow chakra houses our third eye and is the emotional center for our extrasensory perception. An overextended brow chakra can reveal itself in eccentric behavior. An underactive brow chakra manifests itself in nervous and fearful energy.

To balance your brow chakra, and clarify your third eye, sit in a silent meditation. Any visualization exercises will help to clear your brow chakra, but begin by focusing on your third eye itself. Often, when we look at our third eye, it's almost as if it has its own room. Imagine that there is a teeny tiny angel. This teeny tiny angel is a specialist in clearing and cleaning the room that houses our third eye. Imagine this angel knocking on the door of this room, and hear him (or her) announce, "Room service." Then, open the door and let them in. Watch as they work efficiently and effectively to clean every corner of the room. They reach into the corners and gather the cobwebs. They polish the walls, floors, and even the ceilings. Next, they even polish your third eye. Notice how everything is sparkling, fresh and clean. Make sure to say, "thank you," as this small angel hurries off to help someone else.

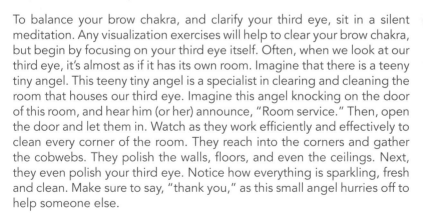

The Crown Chakra

The white crown chakra allows the guidance and wisdom to flow in our minds. Our crown chakra is like a crystal receiver and a two-way communication service. This frequency looks like a white hue of information constantly flowing in and out to the universe. When we receive information from our angels, we are receiving wisdom in a natural, rhythmic flow. Usually, we are as unaware of it as we are of the breaths we take all day long. Sometimes though, this rhythm can reach an overload. There can be a pressure if too much information is coming in; it's as if the brain has filled with ideas and passion to the point where it feels like it might explode. If we don't process the information fast enough, it can lead to a headache. An overextended crown chakra can manifest through mental sensitivities. An underactive crown chakra can manifest itself in chronic headaches.

The next time you feel overwhelmed with ideas, step outside into the fresh air and take a few deep breaths. Fresh air can balance all of our chakras, but especially the crown chakra. Move the fresh air through each of your chakra centers, until it comes out the top crown chakra. Imagine that the fresh air acts as if it were a plumbing liquid that clears clogged pipes. The fresh air moves through any blockages, until everything flows clearly out of the top of your head.

Do you have a hard time going to sleep at night? Do you lay down to try and sleep, and instead, the ideas come flooding in? This can be a good time to get a download of information, and it helps to keep a pen and notebook nearby in case you want to write anything down. But it's not always convenient. Sometimes, our bodies need us to sleep. If this happens during a time when you really need to sleep, try putting a stocking hat on your head. As you place it on your head, think to yourself, "I appreciate the information and ideas, but right now I need to sleep. Please save them for a time when I have more energy to do something about them." The act of putting the hat on top of your head, symbolically closes your divine receiver.

Check in daily with yourself to see if your crown chakra is open and balanced. Closing your eyes, take in a breath and visualize that breath entering into all of your chakra centers, one by one, starting at the root chakra. As it moves through, all of the different chakra wheels spin in synchronicity. Watch it as your breath moves upward out of the crown chakra. Next connect it to your angel. Your crown chakra is now balanced, so trust the love that comes through it.

Our angels operate at a much higher energetic frequency than we do. By raising our own energetic vibration, we are better able to tune into this divine frequency and more easily connect with our angels. As we learn to shift our vibration to a higher level, it will touch our soul and fully connect us to our inner spiritual and creative selves. It will also help the divine download through our crown chakras, become less overwhelming.

Tuning into the frequency of the angels is like tuning into your favorite station on a stereo system. Imagine yourself turning and adjusting a dial on a special device, and this device helps you boost your frequency, thus tuning you in more closely to the angel energies around you. As you find the right frequency, a feeling of peace and happiness settles around you.

Tuning into the frequency of the angels, will help change your thoughts and experiences. It helps us see life from a different perspective. Sustaining and nurturing this frequency will carry us through life and enable us to reach a higher level of compassion and feeling. We will become driven by love for humanity, revitalized by its presence in our lives, and be better able to rise above fear.

As you begin to implement these different angel practices into your daily life, notice how your thought patterns and expectations begin to change. When you place your trust in your angels and let them help you carry some of your burdens, you are simultaneously letting go of worries and fear, and your life will become much more balanced and settled.

Achieving this higher frequency is not difficult. It is as simple as setting the intention. By implementing these angel practices into your daily life, it will start to occur naturally. With this higher level of understanding, our bodies, minds, and spirits will shift into balance. When we reach this shift, we can expect to be more inspired as creativity will flow more naturally. We also begin to feel more like our true selves.

Imagine these three words as the points of a triangle: Body, Mind, Spirit. Now, imagine the triangle is balancing on a stick, that is vibrating at a higher frequency. Your angel is holding the stick and perfectly balances the triangle, and with the higher frequency, it can start to spin. It spins and spins, but as long as your angel is holding the stick, the triangle cannot fall off. Your Guardian Angel is totally and completely invested in not letting that triangle fall.

MEDITATION: WHEN AND WHY?

Now that we've raised our vibration, we are ready to start talking to our Guardian Angels.

An Angel Message

I am your angel for the entire journey; we will spend a lifetime together.
When you calm your mind of the extra chatter, you will see and know
that I am here to give you support in your life.

WHAT IS MEDITATION?

Meditation is the quieting of our earthly thoughts and the focus of intention, asking our angels to see, hear, or feel all of them. We can access the Angelic Realm, simply by being still. Using our extrasensory tools, we can close our eyes to see the heavenly realm. We can quiet our thoughts and the noise of our earthly surroundings to better hear them. We can feel a gentle breeze on our skin and know in our hearts, our angels are there.

Start to think about when, where, and how you will implement regular meditation into your daily life. Trust that by implementing daily meditation, your meditation muscles will grow stronger, as will your faith and bond with your Guardian Angel.

Why Do We Meditate?

Regular meditation helps us strengthen our connection with our angels. Taking time out of our busy schedules on a regular basis makes communicating with our angels a habit. It gives us a formal, structured time to talk to them and check in with them.

Do you leap out of bed in the morning, ready to tackle the day, with your mind already racing about the million things you need to do? Or do you prefer to ease into your day and let the sunshine stretch its rays through the window to help you get out of bed? Do you like to wind your day down quietly? Or are you a night owl that likes to get lots of things done in the twilight hours when the house is quiet. If you are the latter, maybe think about doing your meditation at night. If you are the former, maybe think about working meditation into your schedule during the morning.

Working with our angels daily not only provides us with strength, it releases us from carrying burdens that they are happy to share. It gives us a time and place to release our burdens.

Think about the last time something was really bothering you. Maybe it was an argument with a significant other. Maybe it was something that happened at work with a coworker. What did you do to get over it? Did you talk to your friend? Maybe you went for a workout or a run to get it out of your system. Meditation can also help. Our Guardian Angels are our best friends; they know us better than we know ourselves. Sharing your troubles with them during a time of meditation helps us move through and process situations and life lessons faster.

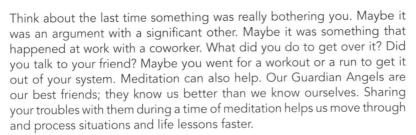

Meditation puts us in a receptive state, making it easier to listen to, and hear, our Guardian Angels. Thus, our connection to our angels becomes stronger and more clear.

Think about a time when you were trying to get someone's attention. Perhaps you had something really important to share with them, but that person was busy looking at their phone, texting or checking emails, and only half-listening to what you were saying. In this day and age, we've all experienced this frustration. Meditation is like putting away your phone and sitting and talking to the person who wants your attention, face-to-face.

In our busy lives, time is a precious commodity. I often hear, "I don't have time to meditate." But time spent with our angels is time worth spending. And remember, our angels always have time for us. Whenever we call, they are there. Dedicating a few minutes each day to check in with them, doesn't seem like that big of a commitment when we remember their availability and commitment to us. By making regular meditation part of our daily routine, we also build in the habit of conversation and a routine of listening to guidance.

Ask your angel to help you find the time. It's simple, just say something like, "I really want to find the time to connect with you, my Guardian Angel. But I need help to figure out how to fit it into my busy life." And mean it.

Routine conversations help the friendship with our angels grow and develop just like any best friend relationship grows and develops. By consciously committing to a daily meditation, we also send a strong message to our angels. The act of commitment tells our angels, "You are important to me, your thoughts and guidance are important to me, every single day."

Commit consciously to a daily meditation. Make a promise to your angels, that you will take time out to meditate every day.

The time we spend with our angels, is time well spent. The more we practice, the better we get. The more time we spend, the faster and more instantaneous the response from our angels. It can be quite shocking when the answers to our questions start to come right away.

As you add the practice of meditation into your daily life, notice how it becomes easier. As you find your way into a routine of meditation, appreciate how every time you meditate, it becomes easier and easier.

MEDITATION: WHEN

In general, the time of day we choose to connect with our angels doesn't matter all that much to them. They are listening always. But the time of day we choose to meditate may make a difference for us. In fact, the angels marvel at the way we measure and mark time, and yet, somehow, time still can linger.

Regardless of when you choose to meditate, it's still good to check in with your angel before your feet hit the floor in the morning. It can be as simple as a single thought to say "good morning." Take it a step further and set an intention for the day. We are especially receptive in the morning.

Think of something simple you could say to your angel every morning. For example, it could be "Good morning. I'm excited to see what the day will bring. Please help me remember to do better at X, Y, or Z."

Regardless of when you choose to meditate, take a few minutes at the end of the day before sleep settles in to check in with your angel. It is a great time to process the day, and clear your head before you go to sleep.

Think of a simple good night you can say to your angel every night, and then pick one or two points from your day to go over with them. Maybe think about your favorite part of the day, or maybe thank them for something they guided you through. Or maybe, unload a worry or frustration if it wasn't such a great day.

An Angel Message

Before you fall into your sleep, we can spend time together and share each other's company. We can celebrate your soul's achievements of the day, and you can burden me with anything you need to unload.
I will bring you good dreams.

Dream State

Between the end of the day and the beginning of the next day, there is a cosmic dance that unfolds. Your Guardian Angel stays near as you sleep, filling your heart and spirit with all of the love that is needed to make your hopes and dreams come true.

There are three basic stages of sleep patterns. The first stage helps to purge the overload and unused thoughts from the previous day: thoughts that don't serve you and are not necessary to hold on to. The second rapid eye movement (REM) stage of sleep is where our angels often sneak in some guidance and direction. They call this "automatic connection." It happens most often when we are too close to a situation to shed light on it ourselves. The third stage of sleep begins the new day ahead.

Have you ever woken up in the middle of the night with a brilliant idea? Keep a notebook and a pen near your bed so you can write it down the next time that happens, because that is a direct message from heaven.

MEDITATION: SPACE

Sacred Space

The first step to a successful meditation is finding a place to meditate that is comfortable and quiet. Comfort is key. When we are comfortable, we are better able to pay attention, and we have a better chance of hearing angel voices and feeling the vibrational connection. We will be better able to enjoy the conversation in our thoughts.

Walk through your house, apartment, or regular space. Where do you like to spend the most time? Where are the comfortable spots? Maybe you already have a favorite corner where you like to read. Sit down in different chairs. Which one feels the most comfortable? Wherever you find a comfortable spot, that might be a good place to meditate today. Remember that there are no rules. Maybe one spot will feel right today, another might feel better for tomorrow.

Having a favorite place to sit quietly and comfortable can sometimes be called a scared space. This space becomes a place where we are not affected by negative influences. It's a place where we feel protected and safe. Sitting quietly can help us gain a different perspective. Birds are known to find their place where they can observe and recognize danger. Humans are naturally drawn to places of comfort where we can clear our thoughts with a tural lighting and calm ambiance.

Think about your favorite physical spaces within your own home, apartment, or living space. Do you have a special spot you go to when you need to figure out what comes next in your day? Or maybe there's a special place you go when you need a "time-out" and when you need to let go of something you've gotten caught up in. Acknowledge this spot as a place where you are not affected by negative influences, a place where you feel protected.

 Maybe there is also an item or items that also bring you comfort. Perhaps you have a favorite fleece blanket that never leaves your side when you are home on a winter day. Items of comfort can help amplify the comforting energy of a space. Anything that helps us calm our hearts and minds will only help create a space where we can have a peaceful connection to our angels.

Clearing Space: Physical

But first, before meditating, we need to clear our space. Clutter, both physical and energetic, can be distracting during a meditation. The clearer your space, the clearer and stronger connection you will be able to have with your Guardian Angel.

 Clear the clutter. That is, the physical clutter. Look around your space. Are you in an office or living room? Straighten stacks of books and clear away papers. Tidy up the desk. Maybe you've found a cozy chair in your bedroom. Clear away any clothes that may be strewn about and shut the drawers. Don't worry, you don't have to organize your entire closet, just simply shut the door.

Clearing Space: Energetic

Clearing energetic clutter is important, too. Clearing the energy that surrounds us will polish our auras, neutralize and purify negative energy, and naturally strengthen our connection to our angels. There are a lot of different ways to clear away energetic clutter. Choose the one that is the most comfortable and appealing for you.

Smudge

"Smudging" is the process of burning sage grass to clear a space energetically. It rids a space of old emotions lingering from the past and honors the future with a blessing. Smudging sends a smoke signal to the heavens, alerting them that you have created a sacred space to invite more clarity. It is the Shamanic way to clear space. Liquid sage is also available in a spray bottle. For someone who doesn't like smoke, liquid sage can be something good to have on hand to help clear your space.

To smudge a space, purchase a smudging stick. A smudge stick is a bundle of sage leaves, tightly wrapped with string to hold them together. These can be found online, at your local metaphysical shop, or sometimes even your local co-op or natural foods grocery store. Or smudging can also be done by burning sage leaves (found on the spice shelf at the grocery store). Light the leaves in the bowl (make sure the bowl is one that can hold the heat of a fire, and don't burn yourself!). Or light the end of the smudge stick and hold it over a bowl (to catch the ashes). Allow the smoke to move out and dissipate throughout the space.

Set an intention to clear the negative and invite the positive. It can be general, something like, "I hereby break up and release all of the negative energy in this space. May peace, light, and love be ever present." Or your intention can be more specific, "I hereby purify this space to allow for a divine connection between myself and my angels." It can even be something as simple as, "Please clear this space." If you speak words from your heart, know that you can't go wrong.

Incense

Burning incense is another way to clear the energetic clutter of a space. Incense sticks can be purchased at metaphysical shops and even at your local co-op or natural foods grocery store. There are many different kinds and combinations. Different scents will have different purposes. For example, frankincense and myrrh will hold a higher frequency the longest length of time. Or you can even find incense sticks that relate to specific chakras.

Find a collection of incense sticks at your local metaphysical shop or even at your local co-op or natural grocery store. Standing in front of the selection, close your eyes. Ask your angel to help you pick something out. Ask them to help pick something that would be good for you, your space, and your connection to them, your Guardian Angel. Then, open your eyes and look at the selection. Are you drawn to pick up a certain package? Smell it. Does it smell good to you? Maybe a different one smells better. Pick the one that smells and feels right to you, and know that your angel helped you pick it out.

Oils: Diffusers and Sprays

There are a lot of different oils and scents that can be used to facilitate and address lots of needs from clearing space to calming our energy. They are becoming more and more common on the consumer market as people look to alternative, more natural solutions for different needs. There are too many to name, but they can all be helpful for various things.

Find a display of oils at a metaphysical shop, or even your local co-op or natural foods grocery store. Take some time to smell different oils and different combinations. Find and choose your favorites. Your favorite scents will lead you to the oils that are right for you. Also, pay attention to what "feels" right when you select different scents to smell, and know that your angel is helping to guide your choice.

Florida Water

Florida Water has been used for centuries as a refreshing tonic and cologne. But its properties are also extremely effective at cutting and clearing negative energy. Florida Water is an ideal method for cleansing space, for those that do not wish to use, or are bothered by smoke. Florida water is actually from Peru. However, its unique blend of essential oils was said to invoke the benefits of the fabled Fountain of Youth, which was said to be located in Florida.

Florida Water can be purchased online or at a metaphysical shop. However, be warned that this is usually sold in a very high concentration, and if you are an extremely sensitive person, straight Florida Water will be much too strong. To use Florida Water as a way to clear space, find a small- to medium-sized spray bottle. Make sure it is one that sprays in a mist, not a stream. Add a few tablespoons to the bottle, and fill the rest with water. The mixture will turn from clear to cloudy. If it is too strong, it will turn a milky white. You want it to have a slightly cloudy color, not milky white. Keep adding water until you get the color right. Use it to spray around your space and house and notice the fresh, clear feeling it leaves behind.

If you are feeling weighted down by negative feelings, try adding a few drops of Florida Water to a bath and take a soak. Let the water wash away any of the negative feelings, and then be sure to watch the water go down the drain when you let the water out of the tub.

Meditation: How to Meditate (Finally)

Now that we've talked about the time of day to meditate, finding a space to meditate, and clearing our space before we meditate, we finally get to talk about how to meditate.

First, we need to quiet our thoughts and allow the daily chatter to melt away. Humans tend to complicate the lines of communication. Sometimes, it is hard to slow the thoughts of our physical world enough to access the Angelic Realm. Sometimes, we have too much on our minds—like that project for work, that party or event we need to plan, or errands to run and grocery lists to make. Our angels want, more than anything, to connect with us. By giving them a chance, they will help us calm the daily chatter in our minds, so we can better tune into them.

Sit quietly and close your eyes. Take a few deep breaths, visualizing these breaths going in and out. Let them calm the chatter and quiet your thoughts. The busier the day, the longer this might take. Don't scold yourself or get frustrated if random thoughts continue to pop in your head. For example, maybe you remember you need to schedule an oil change, or forgot to text someone something about work. As these thoughts come in, gently escort them out by telling yourself to think about it later. You can always ask your Guardian Angel to help you if you are worried you will forget. Maybe even visualize your angel writing the thought down on a clipboard, and ask them to read you the list later.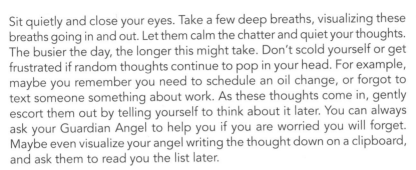

If you find it especially hard to quiet your thoughts, give yourself five minutes with a pen and paper first. Write down everything in your brain that you need to get off your mind before it can be quiet. With practice and habit, your thoughts will be able to become quiet, much more quickly.

There are also tools that can be used to help us quiet our thoughts. Chimes, bells, and Tibetan bowls are often used to change the energy of a space, raising it to a frequency that will serve to awaken our angels and bring a sense of connection to them.

The next time you are ready to sit quietly and invite a conversation with your angel, try marking that moment of silence with a sound. Ring a chime or a bell, or use water in a crystal bowl and make it sing. Think of this simple sound as a way to announce to your angel, "Hello. I am here. I am ready to listen." Stop and notice. Does it invoke a feeling? Perhaps it will suddenly make you feel as if, "All is well."

A crystal glass half filled with water can also raise the frequency in the room and notify your angels you are ready to talk to them. Run your wet finger around the edge of the crystal glass to create a stunning sound that bounces off the walls and melts blockages away in stagnate areas of your home and within yourself.

We can also capture this same feeling by using our voice with a simple chant. For centuries, a single word has been chanted, over and over again, to mark the beginning of meditation. This word is "om." Simple and tonal, it is a powerful word that vibrates with an energy of its own and creates a sound that universally invokes respect. Repeating this simple word over and over creates a mantra. In turn, this chanting mantra heightens the awareness of the mind, body, and your spirit. It brings us to center and focus. Center and focus brings us closer to the higher realm of the angels.

The next time you are ready to sit quietly and begin a meditation, experiment. Try chanting the word "om." Repeat each "om" slowly, dragging out all of the sounds of the word into an "ooohhhhhmmmm." Pause and take a breath. Keep repeating the word until you feel the center and focus.

A Mental Sacred Space

When we are in a meditation, sometimes it is helpful to go to a sacred space in our mind's eye. When our physical surroundings are far from calm and peaceful, we can still create a space in our mind's eye where we can retreat to calm and peace. It can be an imagined place, or a place where we've personally experienced firsthand this calm and peace in the past.

Think about the times in your life where you've been the most calm and content. Perhaps you find peace working in your garden, right outside your back door. Or maybe you have a favorite garden that you like to visit in the summer? Or maybe you've felt the most calm when you were on a vacation in a tropical place and you loved just sitting on the beach and watching the waves. In your meditation, you can "go" to this space where you've felt calm. It might be the dead of winter, but you can still imagine yourself, going outside the back door to sit in your garden at the height of the summer season. Or you can still go back and sit in the favorite park you visited as a child. Go there now and "see" it in your mind's eye. Know that you can "go" to this place whenever you need or want to visit it.

Create your very own angel garden. Go to your mind's eye. If it's daylight, look up at the sky. Are there fluffy white clouds? Do they form into shapes or symbols? If it's twilight in your angel garden, maybe lights are strung from tree top to tree top and the essence of your favorite flowers fill the air. Perhaps there is a bench, with comfortable pillows. Maybe you and your angel could sit there to visit. Perhaps a fire pit will automatically light up to warm you if you get chilled. Create a special garden and hold it in your soul. It can be a wonderful, magical place to visit once in a while.

An Angel Message

I will keep listening to what is on your mind.
We can share time together; just hold my hand and believe in me.
I love our walk and talks. These emotions that we share through
all of our life together is the catalyst to create joy.
I promise to be there and to spend these moments
connected to you.

TOOLS AND CATALYSTS

The metaphysical world has a lot of tools and proven catalysts to help us tune in our extrasensory perception.

Crystals—Prisms

Rainbow energy is highly effective in clearing old, stagnant energy leftover from the day before. Hanging a crystal in your window can throw rainbow colors all over the room when the sunlight hits it just so. The beautiful prism of light can bring a sense of calmness to the indoors. The angels even say that these beautiful rainbow colors are what they see when we humans are happy.

Hang a crystal in your kitchen window. Better yet, hang three together. When you enter the kitchen for the first time in the morning, watch the rainbow lights, dancing through your kitchen. Observe the fresh energy that comes with the start of a new day. Let yourself absorb that fresh energy and use it to help you feel ready to face whatever your day brings.

A crystal also holds the energy of light within it, and, therefore, also carries the color frequencies. This is a connective energy to the Angelic Realm that shows up as prisms of light. This strong energy frequency aids in healing. It can also assist us in accessing our extrasensory gifts by stimulating our intuition.

Hold a crystal prism in the sunlight. Watch the colors scatter around. Tune your senses into the subtle differences. Run your fingers through the light. Do you feel anything? Tune your emotions into the rainbow colors. Do you feel anything? Does your energy shift in response to the colors?

Stones

Gemstones, quartz crystals, Angelite, and lapis lazuli are all stones that we can use to surround ourselves with the natural gifts of the Earth. These are just a few of the gemstone tools that are filled with good energy. Within the gemstones, the healing properties contained in the stone can enhance a peaceful connection to your inner self. When raising the state of conscious we enhance the connection to our angels. Holding the gemstones during meditation can facilitate our natural psychic abilities and assist in the communication with our angels. They can also stimulate body balance, healing, and spiritual growth.

Quartz crystals are stones of balance. The quartz crystal harmonizes the human body's brain waves and is an excellent tool to amplify our inner link to the vibrational energy of the universe. It is a stone that generates power, serving as a tool to enhance, strengthen, and support our energy system. Quartz crystal revitalizes our life force energy, allowing it to expand and promote balance inside of us.

Angelite is a stone of great gentleness, yet strong enough to protect the energy field around our human body. It is an enhancer for spiritual and psychic perception. It can fuel astral travel and amplify telepathic communication. The stimulation from the crown chakra will provide an energy connection to the Angelic Realms. It is a wonderful tool for meditation and promotes spiritual growth.

Lapis lazuli is a beautiful, elegant combination of gold, white hues, and different shades of blue. Lapis is known as a tool for receiving information. The energy flowing from the lapis encourages relaxation and peace and allows us to more easily receive messages that are entering through our subconscious and intelligence.

There are many more stones that can help facilitate our connection to the divine, and different stones can be more compatible with different people's energies. It's important to find the crystal combinations that work best for ourselves.

A book about different crystals and rock categories can be a great place to start. But let your angels help you find the crystals and stones that are best for you.

Find a book or a deck of cards about crystals and gemstones. Flip through and start to read a little about the different properties and qualities of the varied stones. Is your attention called to a specific stone? When you randomly flip it open, does it open to a stone that sounds interesting to you? Or pull a card from a deck of cards about crystals. Does the card sound like something that is appropriate for what you need in your life at that moment? Our angels like to give us a nudge in the right direction when it comes to books and cards. Tune into their guidance and you will find the stones that are right for you.

Play with crystals. Find a shop that sells different stones and crystals and spend some time walking through and picking up each piece. Hold it. Feel it. Does one feel different than another? Tune into the energy of the stone. Does each give off a different energy? Which one feels better?

Grounding stones help to keep us connected to the Earth. They help us to feel safe. Jet is a true mineral for the state of trust and the grounding tree that "roots" us to the Earth. Hematite, tourmaline, jasper, and smoky quartz are also grounding stones.

Find a grounding stone. Pick up different grounding stones, and choose the one that feels the best.

Stones of protection emit an energy that help to keep our auras safe and secure. The different stones for protection are: labradorite, black obsidian, smoky quartz, and amethyst.

Find a stone of protection. Pick up the different stones and choose one that feels right.

Stones that rejuvenate the spirit help to polish our auras and refresh our souls. The different stones that help to refresh us are: rose quartz, diamonds, and Herkimer diamonds. Himalayan sea salt is a mineral that works similarly to refresh us.

Find a stone that refreshes you. Pick up different stones and choose one that feels right for you.

Because stones and crystals are conduits of energy, it is important to clear any old or stagnant energy they may contain before you use them for any divinational purposes. Purifying their energy will reset and recharge them for their new use.

Mix Himalayan sea salt with water to create a saltwater bath. Use it to clear your stones. Gently dip each stone or crystal into the water and let the salt water clear its energy.

Sunlight can also clear and reset a stone or crystal. Place your stones and crystals on the windowsill when it is a sunny day, and let the sunlight purify and cleanse their energy.

Once you've found and purified the stones that speak to you, we can use them to help us. The crystal stones that surround you in your yard, or in your home, conduct healing energy to warm your soul. If the atmosphere is too thick, the stones can help change it. The crystal stones heighten the energy in the space and add a light feeling or shift the ambiance to a calming or brighter energy. Surrounding ourselves with nourishing energy raises our levels of happiness and joy and also adds an energy of kindness to our happiness. Crystal and gem stones help to replenish our energies and strengthen our connections to our Guardian Angels.

Create your own array or gemstone grid. The act of setting up an array or a gemstone grid can be a powerful and immediate technique. First, set an intention. An array of crystals can be greatly facilitated by our intentions.

Next, place the different crystal points carefully in a circular pattern, to send the energy to our intention. There is no right or wrong way to do this. Set them in a pattern that feels right to you. Once you find it, this can be a direct and automatic connection to our angels, and through it, we can receive healing energy in our emotional, spiritual, or physical body.

Candles and Fire

Candles can also be used to calm our emotions and sooth our souls. The image of the flickering flame is a connection to the divine, as is the smoke of an extinguished candle, coiling and rising to the heavens. Candles speak to our solar plexus, our core chakra. It is an image that radiates confidence and inner strength.

Make a wish! Candles are often used in prayer or intention. You can walk into any church all over the world and see rows of candles burning with intention. There is something so symbolic and moving about seeing a row of private prayers burning together in solidarity. The next time you are near a church, if its doors are open, go inside and find the candles. If you are so moved, drop your coins in the box, and light an intention of your own.

Candles are also used in birthday traditions to make a wish. As we get older, these wishes are more sophisticated, moving from the often material wishes of youth to a more dignified intention. The next time you light a candle and go to blow it out, make a wish, just as you would if it were a candle on your birthday cake. Hold the wish in your mind, and blow out the flame. As you watch the smoke curl upward to the heavens, know that your wish was sent along, on its way to your angel.

The light of a candle can also be a tool to calm your heart. Through it, we can soften our gaze and tune into our extrasensory gifts of clairvoyance. Lighting a candle sends a signal to our Guardian Angels. They will recognize that we've just lit up our spirit to gain their attention, and the messages and joy that they will send can be overwhelming.

Light a candle. Begin with a devotion to the heavenly Angelic Realm, and ask to gain wisdom or enlightenment. It can be a specific intention where you ask for guidance about a particular situation, or you can keep it general and vague. Stare at the candle's flame. Watch the flame dance and flicker back and forth until you lose yourself in its dance. What do you see and learn during this quiet, introspective moment? How has your mood changed from when you first sat down until the time you finish?

Pendulums

A pendulum is another tool that can facilitate communication with your Guardian Angels. A pendulum is visual validation that communication is, in fact, happening with your angel. Pendulums can be purchased at any metaphysical shop, or you can even make your own. Simply use a favorite stone as a weight, and attach it to a string or chain. Make sure to purify it by clearing its energy with salt water or setting it in the sun before you use it.

Begin by centering yourself. Grasp the top of the chain or string with your thumb and forefinger, allowing your pendulum to swing easily back and forth with a light momentum. Your pendulum is now ready to react to energy. Ask your pendulum to show you a "no" response. It should swing one direction or the other. To verify, now ask it to show you a "yes" response. It should swing the other direction. Your pendulum is now ready to answer "yes" and "no" questions.

Dowsing Tool

A dowsing tool is another tool you can use to connect and communicate with your angel. Energy makes the dowsing tools respond and move back and forth for a reaction, just like the pendulum. However, dowsing is very reactive and susceptible to different vibrations. It's important to clear away other energy before using a dowsing tool.

Use one of the methods previously discussed to clear away energetic clutter before beginning. Keep your intention and focus while using your dowsing tool, and use it to answer "yes" and "no" questions.

Pen and Paper

Writing in a special journal is another way to directly communicate with our Guardian Angels. The act of putting thoughts onto paper can help us relax our minds, thereby strengthening our relationship with our Guardian Angels. It allows our earthly selves to get out of the way. The act of writing also implies an intention to get lost in our thoughts, and this in turn opens our internal connection. We can become more receptive and can even feel the communication take on a life of its own.

Get a new notebook or special journal and dedicate it to your angel's messages. Find a comfortable space to write. Before you begin, organize your thoughts and any questions you may have for your angel. When you pick up your pen to write, begin by writing your questions or angel topics at the top of the page. Then, letting your thoughts flow freely, write down whatever pops into your head regarding your topics and questions. Did you get an answer or solution?

For this next free-writing exercise, take a minute before you begin writing to center yourself. Try to clear your mind of any earthly thoughts, like grocery or "to-do" lists. Set a timer for fifteen minutes. Next, pick up your pen and start writing on your paper. Continue writing whatever comes into your head—even if it's that grocery or "to-do" list that popped back into your thoughts. The important thing, is to just keep writing until the timer goes off. Next, take a few minutes to close your eyes and center yourself again. When you are ready, read your list. What did your angel have to say today?

The above writing exercises are intended to gain guidance and instruction from our angels. But we can also do writing exercises to tell our angels whatever we need to tell them. By writing something in a journal or in a letter, or even a note file on our computer, these writings will become a personal journal. The result will be a blessing of personal closeness and connection to your angel.

If you've started an angel notebook, use it. You can also start a file on your computer, or write a letter. But this time, instead of asking your angel for guidance, tell your angel whatever it is you want to tell them. Maybe share a triumph from your day. Maybe share an emotion about a certain situation. Through this notebook or journal, you can unload burdens and share your successes with your angel.

Take out a pen and a nice piece of paper. Placing the pen in your dominate hand, begin by writing anything that is on your mind. For instance, how is your body feeling today? Write for one minute. Next, place the pen in your non-dominate hand and write the same message. How is your body feeling today? Write for one minute of time. Compare the two messages. One may be legible and the other, while not clearly legible, is just known because you wrote from your heart.

Automatic Writing

Automatic writing is the process of writing and recording thoughts that do not come from the conscious thoughts of the writer. All of the writing exercises above are designed to help access the realm of automatic writing. Through automatic writing, we can channel messages from our angels.

Clear your thoughts and center yourself by breathing in and out, slow and deep. As you pick up your pen, imagine yourself switching on a light switch. This switch opens your channel of communication to your Guardian Angel. Now write for as long as you need to. These messages can be short and light, or very deep and matter of fact.

If you have trouble with this exercise, try it using your opposite hand. If you are right-handed, use your left. If you are left-handed, use your right. Don't worry about neatness or correct pronunciation. Get out of your own way, and trust the messages that appear in front of you, in written form.

Angel Cards

There are a lot of different kinds of divination cards available. Most people are familiar with Tarot cards. In my opinion, Tarot cards can be confusing and tend to lead to the wrong message. Angel decks include different pictures and messages from angels. As humans, we tend to be visual. Using a deck of angel cards fulfills this visual need.

Shuffle your angel deck. As you shuffle, consider your intention. Maybe you need reassurance about how you are handling a situation. Maybe you need help finding a solution to a problem. When you have finished shuffling your deck, set it down and fix your intention. Get rid of everything else in your mind, for the moment anyway. You can always reshuffle and set a new intention if you need guidance about more than one topic. Pick your card. Use the deck's guide to help you interpret the meanings and symbols of the card and how it applies to your intention. *Or*, forget about the guide, and use your own intuition to interpret the symbols on the card and how it applies to you.

HONORING OUR ANGELS

Altar

We usually think of altars as something found in a church. But making an altar for our Guardian Angel is another way to boost that angelic connection. Dedicating a space to your Guardian Angel is a visual commitment that your angel is important to you. It gives you a specific place to come for assistance—or simply to say, "Hello." Combining some favorite and significant items together in one dedicated space will create a positive, divine energy in that space, thus making it easier to connect to the Celestial Realm.

Make an angel altar. Find items that are significant to you and symbolize your connection with your angel. Maybe find an angel card, picture, or statue to use. You can even use a Bible. Do you have a special stone or crystal? Or how about a feather you've found? Do you have a favorite flower? Combining these favorite things together in a dedicated spot will generate positive and good energy, thereby boosting your angelic connection. Your altar doesn't have to look like an altar at church. It can be a corner of your desk or dresser. It's enough that *you* know it's an angel altar.

If an altar doesn't feel right to you, keep it simple. Angel figurines or even artwork can serve as a visual reminder that our angels are there watching over us. Like an altar, these pieces also serve to honor the presence of angels in our lives, a mental reminder that we are not alone—a symbol that we invite the magnificent angels and their divine energy to be present in our lives.

 Maybe you already have an angel figurine or a piece of art featuring an angel. If so, look at it and study it. Does it invoke a feeling of peace and calm? Maybe it even generates a feeling of awe. If you would like to add angel artwork to your home, look for these characteristics in the pieces that you find. Next, find the perfect placement. Inside or outside our homes, angel figurines or artwork can serve as symbols of love, compassion, and protection.

Distress Call

The private connection to our angels includes blessed guidance in times of trouble and stress. The added pressures we put upon ourselves automatically sends alert messages to our angels, putting them on notice when we need assistance.

 The next time you are stressed or troubled, pay attention. Perhaps you are worn out and need a burst of energy. Perhaps you have a deadline approaching and need a really great idea before it arrives. Think of your stress or fatigue as a distress signal to your angel and pay attention. Any burst of energy that you get, or guidance you receive, or great idea that pops into your head, is your Guardian Angel's answer.

PART TWO

Troubleshooting

STRUGGLES AND TROUBLESHOOTING

By the nature of our earthly existence, we have struggles and burdens. However, when we tune into the spiritual energy of our Guardian Angels, they can help us carry these burdens.

The next time you find yourself struggling with some sort of burden, close your eyes. Maybe your burden is a situation at work with a coworker. Maybe you are worried about reaching minimum attendance numbers for an event you've planned. Maybe, you are worried about the sale of your home. Whatever the case may be, imagine that problem is something tangible that you can scrunch up into a ball between your hands. Now, put it in a sack. Hand the sack to your Guardian Angel. And watch them, as they take it off to the divine realm where they will unpack it and figure out what to do with it. They can help take care of it or help you figure out what to do next.

This time, use a real piece of paper. Write down your burden or trouble on a real piece of paper. Scrunch it up into a ball and toss it into the fireplace or a campfire. As it burns and turns into ash, watch the smoke curl up and reach the heavens. Know that you've sent your message to the angel realm.

If you are using an angel journal, write your burden or trouble in it. Maybe even write the words, "What should I do?" after you've written it. Have faith that your angels will work out a solution. Over the next few days, pay attention. Do you receive internal guidance about the situation? Do opportunities present themselves? Let go of any expectations you may have regarding the outcome. It's possible, your angels might be able to figure out something better than you ever could have imagined; be open to the options they present.

By asking our angels for assistance as early as we can in the experience, we give our angels more time to figure out different solutions. It is also better to ask before we reach the place where our head is in a mental state of crisis, as times like these make it more difficult for us to see clearly.

As you find yourself moving toward a potential crisis, sit in meditation and clear your chakras. Inhale and exhale. Watch as your own breath moves up and through each of your chakras, spinning each light in turn until it escapes through your crown chakra, connecting you to the Angelic Realm. Aligning your chakras will keep your body and emotions strong and secure as you face any upcoming challenges or times of trouble.

Asking for support from our angels is necessary in order to receive their guidance and instruction. Our angels will join us by the boatload, but first we have to ask and invite them in. They love to join us in prayer; they can feel the heartfelt words. They love to join us in song, as singing invokes emotion. Angels will move mountains for us, if we let them. Angels are in our lives so we can live our lives to the fullest potential and keep doing the great work that we do.

As such, when we face times of troubles, we do so with our Guardian Angels' full awareness of the problems we face. As our emotions grow, either in laughter and song, or sadness and grief, our angels are right there with us.

We can even have an entire team of angels if we want them. We can also call upon the archangels at any time. (More about the archangels to follow.) Angels are multidimensional and can be in many different places at the same time. We all can ask for a team of angels if we want it, and there are plenty of angels for everyone.

An Angel Message

Sometimes we watch you in frustration, seeing your struggles.
We want to help you, we want to carry you, but we cannot
until you ask for us.

It really is as easy as simply asking for help. It can even be a simple word, "Help." The next time you are facing a challenge, remember to ask for help.

But remember, our angels also know what is best for us. Sometimes, the emotions we face through sadness and grief move us towards needed change. Challenges in our lives help us to learn the lessons we need to learn in order to grow. In times like these, the best assistance our angels can give us, is to hold us in peaceful balance while we navigate the turbulence.

The next time you find yourself facing a troublesome or tough situation. Instead of asking your angel for a specific outcome, or to take a problem away from you, consider, instead, asking them to simply hold you in peace as you face it. How does this change the way you face the problem? How do you find yourself treating others as you face this problem?

In the moment the call is heard by the angels, their response is to create the miracle at hand. Instead of holding onto the feelings that may be causing you to feel overwhelmed, trust and have faith that help is on the way. There is a two-step universal rule: *If you can think it, you are receiving it.*

Think it and receive it. The thoughts that come to you immediately after you ask for help are important. Pay attention. Do you feel peace? Hope? Faith? Or maybe a solid combination? Trust those feelings.

LET YOUR ANGEL LEAD

Have you ever heard the expression, "Let go and let God"? We can't possibly know all of the ways our angels are working on our behalf behind the scenes. Often, they may be working directly with our family, friends, and loved ones, or maybe even collaborating with the angels of our family, friends, and loved ones. When our angels are in the lead, let them be. They can see everything from a different vantage point, and they have healthy ways of motivating others or dropping inspirational ideas. The outcome will be better than we could have ever imagined if we just step back and get out of their way.

The next time you ask your angel for assistance in a time of trouble, spend a few minutes thinking about your angel with your eyes closed. Can you see your angel, working on your behalf? Can you see them whispering to your friends and family members? Maybe you can even see them consulting with other angels.

As the miracle of angel intervention is unfolding, be ready to trust your gut and intuitive guidance system. If your intuition tells you that you will have a visitor stopping by for a visit, be prepared for a visitor. If your gut says that you have been working too hard and you need to take a break to recharge, do so.

The next time you ask your angel for assistance in a time of trouble, be extra alert for strange requests from them. Maybe you get the urge to suddenly call a long-lost friend. Do it, because maybe your angel has set something up on your behalf. If one day, out of the blue, you get the urge to just go home and take a nap, do it. Maybe you need to recharge, and a long, unplanned rest is exactly what you need.

Words of wisdom are spoken to us during times of turmoil and trouble. This time when we are suffering from mental anguish, pay attention to the unspoken words that come through your thoughts. Listen to these words with your heart and your soul, and recognize the knowing that comes from deep inside of you. The feeling in your gut, your solar plexus, will let you know what is real and what is not real.

When you are upset and troubled about a situation, meditate. Listen to the words of encouragement that come to you during your meditation. Write them down.

Brainstorm, and make a list of the most positive words you can think of. Start with these: Hope, faith, patience, and then add to your list with any words of your own. Write or type them on a piece of paper. Cut them out so each word has its own piece of paper. Put them in a hat and pick one.

This is the word your angel wants you to hold in your heart and it will help you get through your situation.

An Angel Message

Just close your eyes and call out to me; I am part of your life.
Ask of me, and you shall receive. Close your eyes, open up your heart,
release your fears, and release those tears. I really know your desires,
your wishes, and your life. I know your voice as well as your thoughts,
I know what is needed. Just for one moment, close your eyes and ask
me to see for you. I believe in you; you should believe in me.

FOCUS

Sometimes, when we are facing a serious situation, we have trouble focusing. Maybe the options are heavy and the various options and consequences become distracting. This can pull us into worry and fear about the outcome. When this happens, our angels remind us to "stay neutral" so that our minds can clear and reconfigure. They advise us to keep our minds clear so we can better hear their advice.

 The next time you are faced with a serious situation that comes with serious choices to make, imagine yourself keeping your emotions on the left and holding the tasks to accomplish on the right. Combining them is what can cause those feelings of being overwhelmed. Stay neutral about the outcome.

 Jade is a grounding stone. It is the stone of the visionary. When you are feeling overwhelmed by choices, use a piece of jade. Hold it in your hands to settle your soul. You can also carry it in your pocket for the day. It will remind you to stay neutral, and its presence in your space will help to ground you.

COPING

Learning to cope and to find hope are two of the most generated requests to the angels. Angels take this request seriously and respond to us with assurance that we have the strength within ourselves to handle the present situation. With unconditional love, they are close by to give us a hand.

 Rest your eyes for a brief moment and clear your chakras. Visualize your Guardian Angel's hand reaching out for you to hold. Feel a wave of hopeful energy. Know that your angel will not let you get lost in the stress or shuffled about with conflicting advice. Know that they will guide you to the right path through your extrasensory gifts and your intuition.

Sometimes we find ourselves in situations where we just can't deal anymore. We start to lose hope. Don't. In times like this, we have to find a way to be okay. One suggestion is to be honest with yourself. When we find ourselves losing hope in a situation, that's a sign that we need a good meditation more than ever.

Center yourself, clear your chakras, and focus your intention on hope. Ask your angels to help you cope with the present situation. Ask them to hold you in peace, hope, and faith that everything will be okay.

CRISIS

When we find ourselves in a state of crisis, in these precarious moments, usually, we are most in need of unconditional love.

When you face a time of trial and tribulation, remember your angel relationship. Remember their forgiveness and acceptance. Remember their lifelong commitment to you. Remember that you are not walking your path alone.

REGRET

In the present moment, there are two things that we cannot do anything about: yesterday and tomorrow. We cannot change anything that already happened in the past. We don't know exactly what tomorrow will bring. The only moment that truly exists is the moment right in front of us—the here and now.

Regret is normal because we are human beings having a human experience. We are going to make mistakes and that is a fact. Not one of us is meant to be perfect. What matters is that we learn from our mistakes.

An Angel Message

Come little one, you will get it right this time. Slow down and hear my advice. Together we shall find and keep you on your path.

When you find yourself falling into a feeling of regret, stop yourself. Examine the situation. What is it that you regret? Why? Study it to understand the lesson you were meant to learn. Now, release it, and ask your angel to help you remember not to make the same mistake twice.

We've all had nights where we've eaten too much or had too much to drink. Sometimes, we even hear a little voice inside telling us to stop, and we don't listen. The morning after a night like that can be filled with regret.

Learn from these smaller moments of regret. Learn to recognize that voice that is telling you to change course. Practicing with the smaller moments will help you recognize that voice and maybe listen to it to avoid something bigger in the future.

WORRY—IN GENERAL

Sometimes, thinking about the future brings us worry. That is a normal, human emotion. But we tend to waste a lot of energy when we worry about something that hasn't happened yet. We can't possibly know all of the facts for tomorrow. We are only capable of dealing with one day at a time. And remember, our angels are standing by our sides to help us weather whatever storms we have to face.

Have you ever had that feeling, like something, perhaps trouble, is brewing? This is when our faith has to be the strongest. We have to have faith that we will be able to handle whatever tomorrow brings. We have to have faith in our angels, that they will give us the strength we need. With that faith, we can let go of the worry about tomorrow.

An Angel Message

"Don't worry, be happy." The storm will pass, and calm will come.
I will hold your hand, like always, to guide you through.

WORRY ABOUT OUR WORLD

There are a lot of scary stories being reported in the world today. With social media and instant access to information, our world is as small as it has ever been. When we find ourselves worrying about the future of our world, we need to keep perspective. We also need to take responsibility, but only for the parts that we can control. That allows us to release our worry about the things we can't control. To do that, we need to put our hope, faith, and trust in angels everywhere, that they are doing whatever they can, in whatever corner of the world, to bring us to a greater good.

The next time you find yourself feeling overwhelmed with worry by the state of the world, stop. Think about all of the good deeds you've done in the last week. How many of them got reported in the newspaper or on social media? Probably none. Now think about how many people there are in the world. People everywhere, all over the world, are doing good deeds every day. The bad acts might get the attention, but the good clearly outweighs the bad. The only responsibility you have is to keep doing your own good. Do the very best you can with each day. That's the only part you have control over.

Next, think about your own angel, and how hard they are working on your behalf. The next time you are in a crowd of people, close your eyes. Look at all of the angels, everywhere, helping everyone around you. When you hear about something bad happening, close your eyes and ask that the archangels and special teams of angels be at the ready to assist however they can in times of trouble.

Keep it simple. Sometimes, the more simple the recipe, the better everything tastes. There is one simple emotion that can rise above all others. The Beatles got it right when they said, "All you need is love." Love has the ability to rise above fear and hate. By staying in light and love, we can rise above fear.

The next time you hear of something tragic, sit for a minute. Close your eyes and stretch out your arms. In your hands, imagine a ball of light. Fill it with all of the love in your heart. (Don't worry, love naturally and instantly regenerates.) Have it get bigger and bigger, until it's so big you can't hold it anymore. Send the ball of light and love, up into the air like a balloon. As it floats out into the sky above you, it continues to grow. Send it to the people affected by the scary situation. Have it multiply as many times as it needs to and get as large as it needs to. It can even grow as large as an entire city or country. When your balloon of light and love reaches your intended target, gently bring it down to surround the person or place.

FEAR AND ANXIETY

When we are filled with fear, life is dark and filled with everything that frightens us. Our angels will wait until we are ready and calm, and then they can fill our hearts and heads with hope. This hope will shine like a light to keep us out of the darkness. They will help us find peace.

The next time you find yourself facing the darkness of fear, imagine your angel standing next to you. They are holding a light. It can be any kind: a lantern, a candle, or a funky flashlight. Focus on the light, and let it fill you with warmth and feelings of safety and security. Remember to always do this simple visualization when you are feeling fear. Perhaps, you will notice yourself needing to use it less and less.

A common source of anxiety for a lot of people is fear about the future. When we start to look too far ahead, it can easily become overwhelming.

When you think about the future and find yourself worrying and carrying a lot of anxiety, stop. Don't let yourself look past the next three weeks. Only think about what you need and want to accomplish in the next three weeks. Reassure yourself that you can easily manage the next three weeks.

When you find yourself feeling afraid, ask you angel for a hug. When our angels give us their hand or a hug, their touch can feel like a graceful beam of light energy. This special touch travels quickly to our hearts and has a way of surrounding us energetically.

When you find yourself feeling frightened, take in a deep breath, and count to the number nine as you breathe in. Exhale slowly, again counting to the number nine. The next time you inhale, imagine your angel's wings, wrapping themselves around you. Nothing can get past your Guardian Angel's wings.

An Angel Message

You are protected and you are safe. When you are traveling on this journey, and the road becomes too rough, I will have a way of appearing as if out of thin air for you. When you make a wrong turn, I am there to help you get back on the right track.

LONELINESS

It is normal to feel alone sometimes. Especially, when we are challenging old thought patterns and belief systems. Sometimes, we can feel as if "no one else gets me." When we grow and change, if those we love around us aren't growing and changing in the same way, we can easily find ourselves in a place of solitude.

When you wish you had someone to talk to or when you feel like you need to "see the light," close your eyes. Know and understand that it's okay to change, but not everyone changes at the same pace. When that's happening, stay focused on doing what you need to do for yourself, and ask your angel to help by sending a level of understanding to those around you. And remember, you can only control yourself and how you react to a situation. You can't control what other people are choosing to do. Sometimes, finding ourselves in a place of solitude strengthens our connection to the divine and helps accelerate our growth.

An Angel Message

I am your angel. In this very moment, I am watching you tapping your toe. Your sandal is loose. You are beautiful. Yet, you are lost in your own thoughts with your hands fidgeting. Are you in need of a friend? Call to me. Please realize that this is the best time of all to ask me to move this mountain of worry. Do so, and you can begin to lead in life again. Your feet begin to move to the beat of the music. As you relax, your spirit starts to flow free again. I am your encouragement. You are the motion.

CONFUSION

When we are in this realm, walking in this lifetime, it is necessary that we let go of our soul's previous life existences so as to focus on this one. We naturally don't remember what happened in a previous lifetime, because that would add even more confusion to our present situation. Yet, each one of us has a higher self. Our higher selves carry the knowledge of our entire soul's existence. Sometimes, confusion in our lives can stem from our soul's recognition of something that happened to us in a previous life experience. When we find ourselves in a state of confusion, and we don't know which way to turn, it can be helpful to tune into our higher self before we ask for our Guardian Angel's assistance, because it can help us sort the confusion in advance.

The next time you are feeling confused about a situation, clear your chakras, and find a quiet time and place to meditate. This time, instead of instantly connecting to your Guardian Angel, connect to your higher self. Imagine a beam of light extending from your crown chakra. But before it reaches all the way to the heavens, there is a ball of light. This intelligent light holds the blueprint of your entire life's existence. Acknowledge its presence, and then go on to connect to your angel. By acknowledging that some of your confusion may be stemming from your past-life challenges, you better align yourself and your angel to deal with it.

CHANGE

Sometimes we get to a point in our lives where there is a lot happening. Sometimes, some of it is within our control, other times, it is not. Sometimes, we have to stop and remember to find ourselves. Sometimes, any small change that we make can make a big difference. But always remember, we can't fail at change when we invite our Guardian Angel to assist. With awareness, passion, and purpose, change can't fail.

When you find yourself feeling nervous about facing a change, remember that you now have a whole arsenal of tools within the pages of this book to help you navigate your journey. Stop. Take a few deep breaths. You have learned that you are not alone. You have learned how to calm yourself and clear your energy. You are a stronger person for having learned a few new tricks within these pages. Carry that confidence with you as you embrace the change.

Remember that at every end, there is a new beginning. If we stay focused on the excitement and anticipation of the new beginning, we will be less likely to mourn the end of what has passed.

The next time you find yourself in a life change—perhaps it is moving to a new house or starting a new job—instead of looking back to what has passed, focus your attention on the positive and exciting aspects of what lies ahead. This keeps us living in the moment. Being in the moment allows us the best connection to our Guardian Angels.

Change allows us to grow in ways we could never have expected. Routines can be traps against change. When we get stuck in a routine, going through the same motions day after day, it can be comfortable, but become stagnant. We've all gone through times where we feel like we are "stuck in a rut." If we practice adjusting to little changes, then the big ones will be less overwhelming when they pop up in our lives.

When you find yourself becoming too comfortable, and maybe even bored, change it up. Unplug from your routine and see what happens. Choose one day where you do anything and everything you can differently, just to see what happens. When we unplug from our routines, we can find new passions, and ultimately, our purpose.

If it's too overwhelming to take an entire day and do everything differently, just choose one thing in your regular, daily routine, and change that one thing for just one day. For example, when you stop for coffee on your way to work, order something you've never tried. Or maybe you always sit in the same spot each morning at home to have your coffee. Tomorrow, mix it up and sit somewhere different.

SHIFTS HAPPEN WITH CHANGE

Change brings evolution. It is easy to get caught up in old thought patterns. There are a lot of belief systems imposed upon us by our religion, culture, and our elders. It follows the notion that we are doing something because, "that's the way it has always been done." Challenging these belief systems can also facilitate change. It doesn't have to be dramatic; it can simply be sitting for a minute and taking an inventory of why we think what we think and testing it against your intuition to say, "Does this still feel right with what I know now?"

Take a mental inventory of your belief systems. What still feels right, and what doesn't fit anymore? How can you adapt and change to incorporate the new thoughts . . . and perhaps help evolve the old thought patterns and belief systems?

IMBALANCE

Sometimes, when we feel out of balance; it is because of an ongoing or upcoming shift. One side of ourselves is growing differently than another. For example, perhaps our spiritual mind is growing, and our practical mind needs a little help to catch up. Our angels can help us bridge this gap.

If you are feeling out of balance, and the reason above resonates with you as a potential cause, find a quiet time and space to meditate. Think about where you are feeling imbalanced. Perhaps your spiritual mind has grown in leaps and bounds, and the practical parts of you need a chance to catch up. Visualize the areas that need to grow and call in your angels to help "grow" these areas. Visualize your practical side puffing up until it is the same size as all the other parts. You have now given that side of you, room to grow. Next, ask your angels to send you the information and signs you need over the course of the next few weeks to help the practical part of you grow. When you see enough for yourself, it will be easier to believe. It is okay to ask for this; our human brains are naturally skeptical, and our angels want us to use the tools we've been given to believe, know, and trust their existence.

Sometimes when we feel out of balance, it is because we are spending too much time and attention in one aspect of our lives. As humans, we can get absorbed and pulled into ideas and activities that feed our passions. Sometimes we can get distracted and lose sight of other important parts of our lives. It is important to strive for a balance in our lives, so that if we give attention to one element, we don't neglect others. Don't lose sight of what you are doing and what's important in your life.

Think of the most important areas of your life. In front of you are a number of different balls. Assign one ball to each topic. For example, maybe the topics on each ball include: family, friends, career, two or three favorite hobbies or pastimes, or maybe volunteering for an organization you feel passionate about. These balls may be different sizes, depending on the topic's level of importance in your life. Now, know that you are a master juggler. You've been granted this status and no one can take it away. You can juggle lots of different balls at a time, even when they are different weights and sizes. Next, take all of the balls and throw them up in the air, and watch them dance. Instinctively, you know exactly how to move so that you don't drop any of them.

Uh oh. Now one of your balls dropped out of the sky. This could happen for a few different reasons. Maybe, it's something that used to be important to you, but now it's not. Feel free to toss that one away. Maybe a new ball needs to take its place. Another reason this ball fell could be that one of the other balls is taking too much time and attention. It grew without you noticing, and now it is throwing off the delicate and intricate juggling act. Is that ball still important? Maybe that ball needs to shrink in size a little, so that there is still room for the one that dropped.

EMOTIONS

Emotions are the body's way to signal a reaction in response to a situation. Sometimes, our emotions are so strong, they can be difficult to understand and control. Sometimes, we can be accused of "over-reacting." When feelings are strong and stirring to the point where we (or others) are physically affected by them, we need to move these emotions safely through. Angels have emotions and moods too, and they can help.

When you feel like you have overreacted to a situation, take a few minutes to look at your response. Your angel is full of guidance and will provide opportunity to flourish through your emotions, and they will do so with love, understanding, and affection.

In a time where you are calm and quiet, tell your Guardian Angel that you know they accept you and love you for who you are, and thank them for their unconditional love. But ask them to always be by your side during the emotional times. Ask them to provide wisdom and insight during these times to help you balance your emotions.

ANXIOUSNESS

We all feel anxious every now and then. Feelings of anxiousness can come from a lot of different places. It could be an angel vibration, warning us of a danger to our energy field. It might also be anxiousness coming from someone else. Empathetic people often feel emotions from others, and these emotions can easily travel from one highly sensitive person to the next, very rapidly. Either way, it is important to protect our own energy fields. Foreign energies can interfere with our aura's mesh, the part that supports and holds the auric field in place. Interference can cause us to lose stamina and become drained. Angels can quickly increase their support and protection when we are faced with overwhelming feelings of anxiety, or when we need to quickly respond to something important.

When you are overwhelmed by feelings of anxiety, use your logical brain to help you analyze the source. Is the feeling coming from someone else? Or is it a warning meant for you? Ask for your Guardian Angel's assistance. Use your intuitive skills and extrasensory perception to determine which one feels right. If it is energy from someone else, allow it to melt away. If it is a warning for you, your Guardian Angel will follow up with instructions about what you are supposed to do.

Whatever the case may be, it is important to reinforce and protect your own energy field and secure your boundaries. This is as simple as visualizing everything locking together with a protective shield. Feel a sense of warm comfortable energy moving through you as your Guardian Angel helps clear your energy field and reinforce the protective exteriors.

SADNESS/SORROW

When we are sad, our angels are right there with us to help us handle our sorrow. Grief is a normal human emotion, and sometimes we just need to allow it to move through us in order to release it. The love from our angels during this time is gentle and very soothing and also very private. Your tears and emotional pain pass quickly through the ethers to the Angelic Realm. By grieving, we naturally open our hearts to receive unconditional love.

In times of sadness and grief, we don't need to do anything special to reach out to our angel crews, we only have to let ourselves be sad. Crying releases emotion; it's okay, and even good, to cry. In the moments after your tears, tune into the emotional release that you feel. It can feel like you have taken a good, deep, clear breath. Know that this is exactly the moment that our angels wrapped their arms (and wings) around us to give us a hug.

DEPRESSION

Those suffering from depression will tell you that depression creeps in unexpectedly. Normal grief and sadness become slowly amplified. Sometimes, those suffering don't realize they are in the throws of it until it is overwhelmingly unbearable. Your feelings are raw, your heart physically hurts, and facing each day is an incredible burden. While our angels are walking along next to us during this time, they could also use some reinforcements to help bring some sunlight into our hearts.

Energy healers can help bring in armies of extra angels to help us heal our hearts and souls. They can help us to balance our perception. Ask your own angel to help you find the right team of energy workers.

LOST

Our Guardian Angels are patient. They will wait for us as long as they have to. When we become lost, or stuck in our life journeys, they are accepting of us and hold us with compassion. Eventually, our wounded spirits will have no more excuses. We can get "unstuck" when we stop letting these wounds control our lives and allow healing to happen. This makes room for love to return.

 You can hold onto your pain as long as you would like to. It can be for twenty minutes or twenty years; the choice is up to you. Your angel will have patience to wait for that moment. When you are ready, your angel will be with you, and you will take the next step together.

An Angel Message

Take the time now to heal. When the tears dry up,
there will be a shift in a new direction that will set you into a new
motion, and a spark of inspiration will unfold. This is the moment I
have been waiting for! I am here with you. I am still strong for you.
We will take the next steps together, one step at a time.

DEATH

We all know that death is part of life. There is no escaping death. But when a loved one passes, our hearts can break. The loss of someone close to us can leave us feeling empty and alone. Our grief can be overwhelming. Unfortunately, there is not a map or set of directions to navigate the unchartered waters of grief. Every single person grieves differently, in their own way. When we find ourselves dealing with the loss of a loved one, there is nothing we can do but set forth on our own personal journey through the grief.

 When someone we love passes, remember that each person has their own angels, at least one guide, and is directed by a higher self. Trust that team. Visualize the soul of your loved one being greeted warmly by this special team and escorted and accompanied to heaven—the most beautiful place anyone could ever imagine. Your loved one is not alone in this amazing place. Remember, they are surrounded by angels and any of their own loved ones who have gone before.

 When someone we love passes, remember that your own angels are still, always and forever, there for you. They will never leave your side during your entire lifetime. They will help carry you through the grief. They will show you the way.

Remember that even though someone we have loved is physically gone from our world, their spirit has moved on to the heavenly realm. Heaven is a higher dimension, one we can't fully understand. In this dimension, our loved ones can watch out for us, look over us, and sometimes, even talk to us. Our connection with our angels—who also exist in the heavenly realm—can help us continue to stay connected to our loved ones, even after they've passed from this world to the next.

Remember that death brings us the gift of awareness. When someone dies, we learn to value our days. We find ourselves appreciating life. We remember not to take our days for granted, because time on Earth does not last forever. The gift of awareness is an automatic connection to the heavenly realm.

SICKNESS

When we are sick and asking our angels for help and assistance, sometimes our illness can interfere with the angel connection, and it may seem like their responses are more subtle than usual. But they can still send us signs meant to give us inner strength. Sometimes, when we are sick, our angels prefer to come to us while we are sleeping. They can work while we are resting and sleeping.

When you are sick, never stop asking for your angels to help you heal. The more we ask, the more they can do. Remember, they may be helping us while we are sleeping. Visualize them standing by your side while you sleep, doing their best to help you while you rest.

When you are sick and need reassurance from your Guardian Angel, try to remember that during times of illness, signs from our angels may be subtle. Pay attention to everything so you can catch the subtle signs.

INJURY

Our Guardian Angels can help us when we are injured. There are even special angels who just do healing work. We can connect to this special healing angel team through our own Guardian Angel. We can call upon the healing energy of angels at any time.

The next time you are suffering from an injury, visualize yourself showing and telling your Guardian Angel all about it. Ask for their guidance. Maybe they will show you something you can do on your own to help it get better. Maybe they will take your request to a higher level and contact the special healing angels.

Consider scheduling an appointment with an energy healer. Energy healers use this special team of angels on a regular basis. They may have even built up relationships with specific archangels that they call upon to help with a healing.

ANGEL HEALING

Angels operate in miraculous ways, in the purest form of love and a light frequency we can feel. It is so great and strong, there aren't even words to describe its beauty and power. The angels exist in light, and hold unconditional love with every ounce of their being. When we tune into the light and love that they bring, amazing miracles happen. The life force energy generated by our angels is capable of removing energetic blocks in the mental, spiritual, and physical body. The restored balance helps everything run smoothly again.

Utilizing angels in healing can come through many different channels. By stepping out of the way of the outcome, we can ask the angels to assist with the healing process. When intention aligns with the desire to change, and we believe in the possibility of a miracle with the fullest of faith, healing can and will happen. When we are faced with poor health, illness, or injury, instead of cursing our situation, if we align ourselves and believe we can heal and be healed, we open ourselves to the possibility of a miracle.

The next time you are faced with the challenge of illness, poor health, or injury, don't curse your bad luck. Instead, embrace and accept the challenge. Consider your situation an opportunity for a miracle to take place. Tune yourself into your Guardian Angel. Be ready to follow their wisdom and advice. The more serious the situation, consider asking them to contact the specialty angel healing teams. Above all, have and keep faith that your angels, along with the special healing angels will do everything in their power on your behalf to bring about a miracle.

Connecting with our own angels, setting an intention and visualization enables us to do self-healing work. The more we practice, the better we will get.

Set an intention that you would like your Guardian Angel to help you heal. Visualize the problem melting away, and being replaced with a healthy situation, all around. Allow the angels to step in, and help deliver your intention.

Placing your hands together in the form of prayer is humbling, and energy will begin to flow through them naturally. Feel it and begin to recognize it. The light energy will begin to balance the body and have a calming streamlined effect. Send this energy to where it needs to go within your body by imagining it traveling through your body to the area that needs healing. For example, if your back hurts, imagine and visualize this energy going to the ache in your back.

REMOTE HEALING

Remote healing is the process of asking our angels to send healing energy to others. Together with our angels, we can send the power of their light and love healing energy to others in need. Our angels love when we want to help others. They are always there for us when we ask for their assistance in helping others.

Sit quietly in meditation. Set your healing intention and ask your Guardian Angel for their cooperation. Know that there are two important pieces to this puzzle: yourself and your unselfish intention for someone else, and your Guardian Angel's light and love energy. Visualize your intention combining with your angel's energy, swirling off to envelop and help your intended target.

ANGEL THERAPY

We've all heard it said that "laughter is the best medicine." It's true. Laughter and fun in our lives is incredibly necessary to our emotional health. It is also important in our angel relationships. Our angels have a wonderful sense of humor, and laughter is light energy. They like it when we learn to laugh at ourselves, and when we are not too swept up in ourselves and our daily tasks. They love it when we find innocent joy in our world as we go through our days. Light laughter energy can free our spirit from the mundane and sweep us up in a moment. Surrounding ourselves with fun people and observing the joy that pops up for us throughout our day, keeps us laughing and attracts the fun angels.

Today, make an effort to notice when you are having fun. What makes you laugh as you go through your day? How does laughter affect or change your mood and make you feel? Do you notice how it lifts away the darker, heavier energies that we all encounter at various points throughout our day?

Today, make an effort to seek out and find joy wherever you can. Maybe it's stopping at a stoplight, and instead of letting yourself become impatient while you wait your turn, notice the little girl skipping across the street while she walks her dog. While you are waiting in line to check out at the store, instead of thinking and worrying about the next item on your "to-do" list, watch the baby making faces at his brother. Instead of rushing through your lunch break in a hurry, go sit on a bench for ten minutes and try to spy five things that make you smile or laugh.

We may not be able to change where we are or what we are doing right then and there. But we can change what we give our attention to, what we focus on. When we focus our attention on the good and positive things in our life, the trials and tribulations of our daily life become less worrisome and burdensome.

Today, if and when something bad happens, instead of letting yourself get caught up in the drama of the situation, instantly focus your attention on something good. In other words, look for the silver lining. For example, maybe you forgot your wallet when you went to lunch and had to go all the way back to your desk to get it. But maybe on your way back to get your wallet, you ran into someone you really needed to talk to and hadn't been able to find. Or maybe, you got stuck in frustrating traffic on the way to meet a friend. However, during that extra time in the car, you ended up hearing on the radio that tickets are going on sale for your friend's favorite band.

PART THREE

Signs from Our Angels

By now, we've prepared for our angels, reached out to them in meditation, and honored their presence in our lives. We have also talked about how to call them in times of trouble. Our belief in them has been building as we go. Belief is honestly holding a space of trust in our hearts that they exist and are available to help us. This belief will grow into truth as we receive more and more validation. As our body holds this truth, our confidence, and therefore, our angel connection, expands. Now, it's time to start seeing the proof—that validation—that angels are present in our lives.

Think about the proof you, personally, need to see in order to reach the next level of belief, and therefore, truth and confidence, that your angel exists and is present in your life. Maybe it's help resolving a specific situation. Maybe a physical sign would help you to know they are real. Be assured, you are not betraying yourself to your angel by asking this of them. They want us to believe and know that they are there. They also understand our human nature. They know we tend to be skeptical and cautious; they know we need this reassurance. By asking for a specific sign, we invite them to offer proof, and they will be happy to oblige.

Signs from our angels may be closer than we think. Simply asking our angels for signs can set the conversation into motion. The signs from above are easy for us to see—if we pay attention. We need to notice these signs, because often, they are subtle. But when we ask for a specific sign, and then look for it, we will find validation when we need it.

We've started to tune in more to our surroundings by looking for laughter, joy, and humor. Now, it's time to notice details. As you go through your day today, focus on details you might not normally notice. Look at the clouds. What shapes do they make? Look at the leaves, strewn about the sidewalk. Do they make any special shapes or symbols with the way they are scattered? Look at the shadow of a tree that dances across the sidewalk or road as the wind blows. Does it look like anything special?

There are two critical pieces to recognizing signs and symbols as being those sent from our angels. The first is our attention. Think about when, where, and how our attention is drawn to certain things. Some things we notice, others we don't. That has meaning and intention.

In the previous exercise, we looked for signs and symbols in the ordinary. Think about the signs you saw in the clouds, leaves, or shadows. Think about how your attention was drawn to a certain cloud or a certain tree. Now, think about all of the other clouds and trees everywhere all day that you didn't notice. Because surely, you didn't stop and look at every pile of leaves, all day long. Know that your angel drew your attention to the clouds, leaves, and trees that they wanted you to see.

It's easy to see a sign and dismiss it as something that was "just our imagination." We've probably heard that phrase a lot throughout our lives: "It was just your imagination." However, utilizing our imagination to see shapes and symbols in the daily world is actually a critical piece to seeing these signs, and thus, understanding them as signs from our Guardian Angels.

Think about this: Who talks to us in our thoughts every day, all day? The angels of course. When we use our imaginations to see a shape or sign in the ordinary, we can know that our angels are behind that as well. They send us thoughts through our imagination to make sure we notice the signs they plant for us in our daily path. Our "imagination" helping us to define the symbol that we are seeing is actually a whisper from our Guardian Angel, directing our attention to, and helping us determine, the sign they left for us.

Trust your imagination. When you see something you think may be a sign or symbol from your Guardian Angel, get in the habit of checking in with your gut. Use your intuition to confirm the sign. Say to yourself, "I see a heart when I look at that cloud." Next, ask yourself the question, "Is this a sign?" What resonates within you when you ask? Does your gut answer yes? Does yes "feel" like the right answer? Or maybe your extrasensory perception even heard your angel whisper, "Yes."

An interesting phenomenon is happening in both heaven and Earth. Angels everywhere within the Angelic Realm are becoming motivated and moved to prove to us that they exist. They are reaching out to connect with us in massive quantities. Likewise, here on Earth, people are learning more and more about the Angelic Realm and the roles and purpose of our Guardian Angels. The result is a cosmic shift that is pulling these two realms closer together than they've ever been before. Communication with them is easier than ever, and there are multiple signs that they are in our lives.

Today, count how many things remind you of angels as you go through the day. At the end of the day, make a list of what they were.

After you read about all of the physical signs our Guardian Angels, and angels everywhere, leave for us to see, do the above exercise again and see if that number increases. Maybe you even found some signs and symbols that aren't in this book.

Signs can utilize any and all of our senses, both physical and extrasensory. They are symbols in our physical world that help us connect to the spirit and angel realm. Signs stop us in a moment, and in that moment, we realize a message of significance. It can be a smell that triggers a memory; a random song that pops onto a radio station; a passing billboard with a picture of an angel, butterfly, ladybug, or bird. They are sent to us by the millions, but it is the ones we notice, and the moment that we notice them, that is critical.

Think about different symbols: stars, hearts, feathers, butterflies, birds, or dragonflies. What sorts of symbols resonate with you? The next time you meditate, have a conversation with your angel about signs and symbols. Ask them what their favorite signs are to use with you. Ask them if different signs mean different things.

An Angel Message

You will never be alone. Just because you may not be able
to "see" me, I am still here. I will watch what you watch,
and I will see what you see. I will care about what you care about.
This is how I know what it truly is that you need.

As we learn to recognize the signs coming from our Guardian Angels, a thought is held for just a moment. We can ask our Guardian Angels to show us a specific sign. But we need to be ready to think outside the box when we do.

Ask your Guardian Angel to show you something specific, like an eagle. Perhaps some time during the day, an eagle will soar across our line of sight and we will have easy validation. But did you also hear the Eagle's song playing on the radio when you turned it on? Or how about the statue of the eagle at the gift shop? Maybe there was an eagle featured on a billboard or commercial. Those count, too.

Also, we need to watch for the humor. Our Guardian Angels love to get creative when we ask them for specifics. They will push it to the very edge, just to get us to laugh. They love it when we laugh at something they put in our path for us to see.

Back to the example of the eagle. Did you also see the guy standing on the corner next to the sandwich shop—dressed in the eagle costume, flapping his wings to try to get people to notice his sandwich board?

FEATHERS

Our angels love to use feathers as a sign of their presence. It makes sense, considering angels have wings. Wings come in all shapes and sizes, but no matter the shape or size, they all tend to drop a feather here or there. Seeing a feather is a sign from our angels that specifically reminds us that they are here with us, always. Seeing a feather across our path is a reminder that nothing is too big or small for our Guardian Angels to handle.

Count the feathers you see today. Perhaps you saw a giant feather from a large bird out on your walk. But maybe it was a teeny-tiny, little white feather, like the kind that sneak out from a feather pillow. Maybe you just see one, but it was strategically placed—somewhere you'd never have expected to find a feather. Maybe, you will start seeing them everywhere, in all shapes and sizes. Remember, every angel has a unique and distinct personality; they don't always do the same things in the same way. My angel might use different tactics and tricks than your angel.

An Angel Message

The lightest of a feather that I leave for you, with the hope that
your curiosity is heightened to become a keen observer
of all the signs among you. Today, I leave you feathers, in the hope
that you see the blessings. The feather is from the most beautiful
living creatures gifted with the ability to show plumage . . .
use your talents and gifts to fly high with them.

The following are some common signs and symbols that the angels send us every day. There are also suggested interpretations of what these signs might mean. However, use your own intuition to determine if the interpretation provided resonates with you. Your own Guardian Angel may choose and assign a different meaning to the sign. But don't worry, they will always tell you what it is.

BUTTERFLIES

Sometimes, it is the little things that can get us excited. A small butterfly floats along its day and welcomes itself in and out of the flowers, from the prettiest of the gardens to the stray sunflower that popped up under a bird feeder.

The next time you see a butterfly bustling about a summer day, let it reassure you that you are following your path. But also let it be a reminder from your angels to take notice of the flowers. Stop and smell them, appreciate their beauty and color.

A butterfly is also a symbol of growth and change. It starts out as one creature and becomes another.

When you see a picture or a photo of a butterfly, let it represent change. Let it remind you that you are growing and learning at exactly the right pace. There is a plan for you to some day spread your wings and fly.

Blue butterflies represent peace. When you see a blue butterfly, perhaps it is a reassuring sign that an issue you've been struggling with is finally at peace. Or maybe it means that you have to seek out more peaceful moments in your life.

BIRDS

Birds have a lot of similarities to our angels, so it's natural that they would be a favorite sign sent from the Angelic Realm. Birds spread their wings and fly up and, therefore, have a unique perspective from above.

The wings of a hummingbird move so fast that we can barely see them, and yet, they manage to move through a garden peacefully, finding their favorite flowers and seeking out the sweetness. A hummingbird can be a sign that we need to spread our wings and fly—to just get going and do whatever it is that we've been hesitating to do. It can also be a reminder to keep humming away, and don't forget to find the sweet moments in each day.

Robins are a sign of spring and new beginnings. When you see a robin, perhaps a change, and even a fresh, new beginning is just around the corner.

Eagles are a sign of freedom and strength. Seeing an eagle could mean that you may soon be called upon to be a leader.

Cardinals often represent our loved ones who have passed. When your angel sends a cardinal your way, it is a reminder that your loved one is still nearby, keeping an eye on you from heaven.

Blue jays, while beautiful, don't have the greatest reputation. They are known as bullies and can be mean to other birds. When you see a blue jay, perhaps it is a sign that you need to see the true colors of someone in your life.

Hawks are another bird of strength, but are known for their sharp eyesight. When you see a hawk, it can be a sign that you need to watch your back and keep an eye out. Be extra careful about trusting those around you.

Owls are a symbol of wisdom. When you see an owl, it could be a sign that you have already gained the wisdom you've been seeking.

FLOWERS

The sweet smell of a fresh-cut bouquet of flowers is a vivid reminder that we need to "stop and smell the roses." But different flowers can also represent different signs.

 What is your favorite flower? Why? Do the attributes of your favorite flower correlate to something in your own life? The next time you see your favorite flower, stop and think about what message your Guardian Angel might be sending you by placing it in your path.

 The next time you see a fresh-cut flower, stop and smell it. What do you smell? Does it have an essence? Perhaps it doesn't, but it probably still smells fresh. The mere fact of thinking about it and stopping to smell it reminds us to stop and observe the details happening all around us, all of the time.

 Next, think about how the flower makes you feel. If it smells strong and fresh, does smelling it change your mood? What color is it? Does the color mean something special to you? Does the color change your mood at all? Smelling flowers and taking a minute to appreciate their color and beauty can raise our spirits and give us an uplifting boost of energy.

 The next time you are feeling down and depressed, find a local garden, greenhouse, or arboretum. Spend some time walking through. Let yourself be surrounded by the plant energy and strength. Breathe in the varied smells in each different corner. If you are lucky enough to live in a city with an indoor arboretum, this is an especially energizing activity in the middle of winter. Note the difference in your emotions from when you enter to the time you leave.

SUNFLOWERS

Sunflowers are happy plants. With a beautiful yellow color, they hold up their heads to always see the sunny side of things. It is a strong flower that can grow unexpectedly from a few seeds dropped accidentally under a bird feeder. The flower is a sign of independent strength and a reminder for us to always stay grounded.

 Next spring, plant a row of sunflower seeds in the ground. Watch them grow, taller and taller, always looking for the sun. As summer turns to autumn, notice how they become a staple for hungry birds and animals. The sunflower gives itself away to sustain others.

 Seeing a sunflower as a sign can be a reminder to stay grounded. We can only be strong for others, if we keep ourselves grounded in faith and balanced in our tasks. It can also be a reminder that, as we serve others, we must still take care of our own needs and not give too much of ourselves away.

ROSES

Roses are known as a beautiful, complicated flower. Their smell is among the sweetest, their thorns a contradiction. Their petals are soft and rolled together in complex layers.

Roses can be a sign of love. They can also serve as a reminder: As you get caught up in the beauty of something, don't ever forget about the thorns.

DAISIES

Daises are happy, cheerful flowers. Daisies usually grow together in large clumps, and when we see them at the flower shops, they are usually sold in bunches.

The next time you see a large bunch of daisies, notice how their happy energy is contagious. Let them cheer you up and make you feel better about your day. When your Guardian Angel draws your attention to daisies, know that he/she is trying to cheer you up and make you feel better about something.

TULIPS

Tulips are one of the first resilient flowers of spring to come poking up through the ground. In order to be one of the first flowers to appear, they brave the cooler temperatures. Tulips come in every imaginable color, and fields of tulips have been known to draw tourists and crowds.

Tulips can be a sign of strength in new beginnings. When your Guardian Angel sends tulips your way, know that they are praising and celebrating your strength and beauty. Perhaps you've taken on a new challenge and done well with it. Tulips showing up for you is like your Guardian Angel saying, "Good job."

LILACS

Fragrant and beautiful, lilacs are an early flower of spring. But their presence is fleeting. One week they are filling the trees, the next week they are scattered petals on the sidewalk, not to be seen again until the following year.

When you find yourself admiring the lilacs in spring, stop for a minute and breathe in their amazing essence. Let it swirl through you, from your head to your feet, energizing you with the freshness of the spring season.

 When you see and notice the fallen petals of the lilacs scattered about on the sidewalk, perhaps your Guardian Angel is sending you a message to stop for a minute and appreciate all that you have.

NUMBERS

Whenever we notice repeating numbers appearing together, it's a sign. We usually notice numbers like this when we glance at a digital clock to check the time, and we see that it is 1:11 p.m. or 2:22 a.m. But repeating numbers can pop up anywhere. Perhaps in a hotel room? Or maybe in an address. The holiest of these numbers is 333, and it is said to represent the trinity.

 Do you have a favorite number? What does it mean to you and why? Perhaps you have a lucky number from your days playing on a sports team. When you see it, what does it make you think about?

 When you catch matching numbers on a digital clock, stop and make a wish. Use it as a reminder to send your Guardian Angel a mental reminder about something that you want to have happen in your life.

 When you see the number "1" in repetition together at least three times, perhaps on the clock, for example 1:11 or 11:11, it is a reminder to focus your thoughts on the positive, because that is what you are creating and manifesting.

 When you see the number "2" together in repetition three times, perhaps on the clock, as in 2:22, it is a reminder to us to keep a balance. Specifically, we need to remember to balance our faith, logic, and playfulness. We also need to remember to balance our mind, body, and spirit.

 When you see "333" repeated together, this is the trifecta of perfection from the ascended masters and wise elders. When you see it, let it be a reminder to gather all the information you can to assist you on the way forward.

 When you see the number "4" repeated together, as in "444," it is a sign that the archangels are taking notice of your efforts and encouraging you to keep up the good work.

 When you see the number "5" repeated together, as in "555," it is a sign that there is change ahead, and your direction is about to shift. If you keep noticing the number 5, your Guardian Angel may be preparing you for change and telling you to slow down and pay attention so you don't miss the turn.

The number "6" together, as in "666," is a sign to pay attention to what and where you are focusing your attention. It is a reminder to let go of fear and doubt, and stay positive.

The number "7" together, as in "777," is a sign of strength and courage and a notice to us that our persistence has been heard. Our angels are saying "thank you" for involving them and want to bring you reassurance that you've been heard. They are happy and excited to continue towards new endeavors.

The number "8" together, as in "888," is a sign of infinite abundance. When you find yourself noticing "888" there has been a progression towards abundance, and that flow will continue.

The number "9" together, as in "999," is a symbol that spirituality is a part of your life, as is kindness. It is a sign that elite light workers have a job to do, and to stay in the light.

Perhaps, every time you look at the clock throughout the day, the numbers match. For example, the first time you check the time, it is 1:11. The next time you check, it is 2:22 and so on. Whenever we find ourselves glancing at the clock and the numbers are the same, and it happens several times within the same day, our Guardian Angel is trying to tell us that we are on the right track with something big in our lives.

There are also lucky numbers. Below are two combinations of numbers that have special meanings that are worth mentioning.

When you see the numbers "717" together, it means you have a divine mission. Your Guardian Angels are telling you that you are on the right path. Keep up the goodness, and move forward globally on a larger scale.

When you see the number "818" it means you have earned the right to be confident. You have completed a karmic task and can move on to create new ambitions, with inspiration and abundance.

PENNIES

We've all heard the expression, "Find a penny, pick it up. All day long, you'll have good luck." We've also all seen pennies lost on the ground, left behind because they weren't worth looking for . . . their sum so small that some don't bother to pick them up when they see them. And yet, put a bunch of pennies together and they add up to something. Pennies are also made from copper, and copper is a conduit for energy.

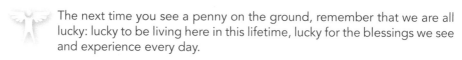

The next time you see a penny on the ground, remember that we are all lucky: lucky to be living here in this lifetime, lucky for the blessings we see and experience every day.

The next time you see a penny, pick it up. The act of picking up a penny sends a very strong message to your Guardian Angel and the universe in general. It says, loud and clear: "Every little bit is worth it."

Use your imagination, and gather together as many pennies as you can find. Stack them up and create something fun. What did you make with your penny creation? A house out of pennies? A bridge? A sculpture? Even something that is seemingly small and insignificant, can be combined with others to create something amazing.

HEARTS

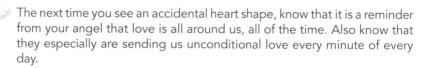

The shape of a heart is a common symbol. We see pictures of hearts all around us every day, and sometimes we don't even notice them. But have you ever seen the shape of a heart that looks as if it were formed haphazardly? Perhaps you came across a leaf, and its shape was a perfect heart. Or maybe amongst the grass clippings scattered on the sidewalk next to a freshly mowed lawn, a few curled together to form the shape of a heart.

The next time you see an accidental heart shape, know that it is a reminder from your angel that love is all around us, all of the time. Also know that they especially are sending us unconditional love every minute of every day.

RAINBOWS

Rainbows after a storm illustrate triumph and peace after turbulence and trouble. The colors of a rainbow also flow in the same order as the chakras: red, orange, yellow, green, blue, violet.

Think about the air after a storm has passed and a rainbow appears. The air after a storm is fresh and hopeful. Seeing a rainbow can be a reminder to clear the air. Families don't always get along; sometimes we weather various storms together. After an argument or disagreement, open up your house; let the fresh air in. Clear the energy by lighting sage or burning incense, and make your own rainbow by hanging a crystal in the sunlight.

If you are out and about and you see pictures of a rainbow, or rainbow colors together, over and over, perhaps your angel is sending you a message that the storm has passed and you can now move forward.

When you are facing a challenge or trouble in your life, and you experience a storm that results in a rainbow, perhaps your Guardian Angel is sending you a reminder. By showing you a real rainbow while you are in the midst of facing a troublesome time, your Guardian Angel is reminding you that, "This too shall pass." There will be better times ahead; just stay strong and weather the storm.

GOOSEBUMPS

We can get signs from angels through feelings in our bodies. Have you ever gotten the shivers? Do you ever get a bad feeling in your gut, like something bad is about to happen? These are signs sent to us by our angels.

We are all familiar with getting the goosebumps; when a chill suddenly spreads across your back or down your arms, and the hairs on your arm stand at attention. Our logical brain may try to process a reasonable explanation: Perhaps there was a sudden draft from the window. But sometimes, especially when there is not a logical explanation, our physical body is connecting to the spirit energy of our Guardian Angel.

The next time you unexpectedly get the goosebumps, know that your angel is nearby. What do you think your angel wants you to know? If the goosebumps come with a shiver of excitement, maybe your Guardian Angel wants you to know that they are excited for you. In the same way, sometimes the hairs across the back of our neck stand up, and our goosebumps come with a boost of adrenaline. Maybe this time, our Guardian Angel is warning us to proceed with caution.

NUDGES

Our angels nudge us all of the time. An angel nudge is one way they get our attention. That feeling you get to look at the clock, and when you do, you see that the time says 3:33 p.m. Or when you "happen" to look up at the sky, and when you do, you see a cloud that looks like a heart. An angel nudge is a flash of inspiration to direct our attention in a certain place, or maybe slow down; or maybe our angel nudges us that we "need to leave right now."

Today, concentrate on the nudges. Learn to recognize when and how your Guardian Angel nudges your attention or directs you to listen. By tuning ourselves into these nudges, we enable ourselves to receive and follow our Guardian Angel's directives on a regular basis. With practice, it will become second nature. The result is that we are not only talking to our Guardian Angels, but listening and following their divine counsel and direction.

The next time a really random thought interrupts you, let it, and listen to it. Write it down if you have to, and then go back to what you were doing. These random thoughts are also nudges. Angels are not necessarily on the same time schedule that we are, but when they have something to say to us, they say it.

COINCIDENCE

It's true what they say: There is no such thing as a coincidence.

The next time you catch yourself calling something a "coincidence," know that it is not. Instead of writing the incident off as a coincidence, look for the connection. What does your Guardian Angel want you to notice?

PHOTOS

Did you know that angels like to be included in your photographs? Have you ever taken a photo, and there is a little drop of unexpected, brilliant light? Sometimes these are called orbs.

The next time you are celebrating something special, take a lot of photographs. Take the same picture, three times in a row. Do you notice anything different in any of the photographs? Do any of them have a little, brilliant ball of light? It can be any color.

TAKE THEM SHOPPING

No matter the situation, our angels love to go shopping. They act as our personal shoppers. Even with the most mundane trip to the grocery store, they will whisper forgotten items in our ear or point us down an aisle we might have skipped, all because something we love is on sale.

Are you someone who only shops with a list? The next time you need to go to the grocery store, try taking a big leap of faith. Leave your list at home. When you walk into the store, let go of any angst you might be feeling because you've walked in without a list, and trust your angel to help you. They will feel honored that you've put your faith in them, and they won't let you down.

The next time you set out on a specialized shopping mission, perhaps you need to find the perfect shoes to go with a dress. Or maybe you need a dress or suit for a special event. Or maybe, you need to find the perfect gift for someone. Sit quietly for a minute and set your intent. Explain to your Guardian Angel what you need. Did you get a nudge? Maybe they showed you a picture of the front of the store, or perhaps they whispered the name of it into your thoughts. Or maybe you have a sudden, instant knowing about exactly where to go.

SONGS

Our Guardian Angels love when we listen to the radio. They send us messages and signs all day long through the songs we hear playing on the radio. Have you ever caught yourself flipping through the radio stations in the car, and catching a song that reminds you of a loved one who passed? Or maybe, every time you turn on the radio, the same song is playing. Guardian Angels also love our playlists. They know that we've already created a list of our favorite songs, and if we set our playlist to shuffle, they can choose the exact song we need to hear in the moment we need to hear it.

Tune yourself into the songs you hear on the radio. Which ones do you notice? Do you feel a nudge to change the channel, and by doing so, do you find the perfect song? By tuning into our Guardian Angel's energy and paying attention, we can learn to recognize when they are speaking to us through song.

Do the lyrics of a song ever randomly pop into your head? The next time this happens, pay attention. Perhaps, your Guardian Angel is singing your favorite song to help you answer a question or to figure out a problem.

Set and keep your playlist to the "shuffle" option. By setting your device to shuffle, you let your Guardian Angel pick the next song for you, and they may just surprise you with exactly the right song you need to hear.

FRIENDSHIPS

Our friendships are absolutely signs and verification that our Guardian Angels are always working behind the scenes on our behalf. Like a giant game of chess, our angels work with other angels to make sure we cross paths with the people we need to meet. People come in and out of our lives at certain times because these are the people we need to meet. By understanding that our angels are helping to coordinate the people who come and go from our lives, we can be thankful and appreciate all that our Guardian Angels do to help us learn and grow.

Think of the most important friendships you've had in your life, most especially, the friends you've made as an adult. What were the circumstances surrounding the way you met these important people? Chances are, you will find a lot of serendipitous moments when you start to look at the way you met certain friends and their correlating significance in your life.

Sometimes, there is no better advice than that of a best friend. We seek advice from our closest friendships because we know and trust them, and they know and trust us better than anyone else. Because friendships like this are orchestrated in the divine realm of the angels, know that this friend is perfectly poised to give you really great advice. Because of this angelic connection, it is almost as if your angel is able to speak through them to you.

 Think about some of the most challenging people you've met in recent years. Sometimes, challenging people cross our paths because we need to go through certain experiences in order to learn our lessons and keep growing in the right direction. Our angels help coordinate relationships to align us with people who can help us learn and grow.

 Think about some of the friendships you've had in the past, but have since slipped away. Think about how those people may have been important for a different stage of your life, and now you've moved on to a different place where you need to have different experiences.

An Angel Message

I can't always explain to you in words the connections we have and feel. It can be the way you view your morning sky, or the way your attention is drawn to a specific billboard after I've nudged you to take a different route. It can also be the words you've heard repeatedly throughout your day. It can be that feeling in your heart that makes you feel like everything will be okay. And it will be, because I am connected to you, forever and always.

REFLECTIONS

Now that we have come this far together, and before we go into the next section, let's take a moment to pause and reflect.

 Take a moment to look in the mirror. Really take a good look at yourself. Do you see anything different? Focus on the comfortable feeling that is starting to wash over you. We are all complicated. We all have many different sides and faces that we show to the world. But through all of those different sides and faces, your personal Guardian Angel is closely connected to you, your understanding of yourself, and your outlook on life. They know every question; they know every thought. They try always to answer your questions and be your support through every thought. This moment, right now, is only between yourself and your angel. Let yourself smile. And know that your angel is smiling with you.

PART FOUR

Go Forth

A shift is happening. As we learn to raise our vibration and connect to the divine realm in order to become more present with our Guardian Angels, we are changing and growing. Because we have let our angels into our life and hearts, our thoughts naturally become kinder and more positive. This shifts our energies.

These new exceptional energies are held in the color frequencies of golden and violet tones. These rich colors hold the natural knowing of compassion and truth and sensitivity. This is part of the chain that will bring in kinder and more polished energy to our world. By simply being you, you are making the world a better place.

By implementing some of the practices in this book, what has changed for you? Perhaps you have become more observant? Be aware of your kinder thoughts. Be aware of how your patience for others has grown, now that you have a better understanding of different energies and how to keep your own heart calm. What are some other changes you've noticed?

Our Guardian Angels dedicate a lifetime of servitude and support, and don't ask too much of us in return. They simply ask us to "go forth." Our angels give to us so that we can give to others. Because we have let them into our lives, as we go forth, we will naturally use our time and talents to help ourselves and others. Our angels are already guiding us to the right path and helping us to make the best decisions. When we follow our hearts and the guidance of our Guardian Angels, we will simultaneously be making the world a better place and helping to raise its vibrational energy.

Play with the idea of "paying it forward." When you carry yourself in a kind and compassionate manner, watch the effect on other people. You don't have to buy everyone coffee or spend a lot of money. Instead, just start small. A simple smile should do it. The next time you are at a coffee shop or the grocery store, smile at three people you don't know. What happens?

Today, make an effort to make friendly eye contact with the people you pass on the street. Notice the power in this simple act. By looking someone in the eye, you are acknowledging that you "see" them. How does this make you feel?

Our angels don't ever want to tell us what to do. While they are there to offer guidance and support, they do not want to give us a set of instructions or directions. We are here to have a human experience, we are here to fully and completely utilize our own freewill and make our own choices about how to live our life.

With that said, there are a few simple principles to keep in mind, and doing so will make it easier for us to go forth and live a happy, purpose-filled life.

The tips of my wings reach out for you when you are searching
for your purpose. That feeling of a breeze you get on the nape of
your neck? I am up in the air helping you with your worries and concerns.
Tell me what you think and tell me all that is on your mind.
I am your angel for all time. I remind you to take a vacation when you work
too hard. I remind you of timely moments to pay attention to.
I won't forget. As I pass by I see the old you, and the new you.
I know what to expect and I know how to amaze you.
And, I am always awestruck by the way you keep moving forward
and make a difference.

BE KIND

When we make a difference in someone else's life, it is like inviting our Guardian Angel to align our day. Always remember that our Guardian Angels know a lot more about what's going on in the world than we do. They have the behind-the-scenes perspective, the bird's-eye view. A simple act of kindness, something that takes hardly any effort for us to do, might mean the world and make an enormous difference to someone in need.

We've already talked about doing this in different ways, but pay attention to the random thoughts and directives, the pulls that come out of nowhere. For example, perhaps you get the urge to use a different exit and take another route home. As you come to the stoplight, you see a homeless man with a sign, begging for food and handouts. Your eye glances at the granola bar lying on the passenger seat that you felt compelled to grab and meant to eat for breakfast on the way to work. When you hand that granola bar to the homeless man, maybe he starts to cry because he's really hungry, and it's the first time someone showed him compassion all day. That simple act of rolling down your window and handing it to him was an easy act of kindness on your part, and meant the world to him.

Like attracts like. When we are kind to others, they are kind to us. When we deliver words with a smile, words with a smile are more likely to be returned. By carrying ourselves with compassion and going about our day with kind words, we draw that energy back towards ourselves.

The next time you are out at a restaurant, watch and observe how others are treating the wait staff. Notice that when someone is rude and complaining, the body language of the staff becomes stiff and formal. When someone is relaxed and caring, the staff responds similarly.

This does not mean don't stand up for yourself. When we carry ourselves through our day with care and concern for others, there is still a chance that we cross paths with someone who is miserable and out to spread their negative feelings among everyone else.

When we cross paths with someone intent on spreading negative energy, there are a few things we can do to block it. First, set up a protective shield and ask your Guardian Angel to keep it safe. Ask that their negative energy reflect back, and not be absorbed by your energy This is especially important if you identify with being an empath and easily or accidentally take on other's emotions as your own. Next, take the high road. You may not be able to control how someone else is reacting in a situation, but you can always control your own actions. Let your Guardian Angel guide you up to the high road, where you can get through the situation and be proud of yourself for the way you handled it.

BE POSITIVE

There is power in keeping our thoughts clear and focused on the positive. First and foremost, as stated above, like attracts like. By staying positive, we attract other positive people in our lives. Positive attitudes raise us up to a higher level, energetically. Negativity drags us down to the lower levels. When we tap into our connection with our Guardian Angels, it is hard not to stay positive. With hope and faith in the divine, we know we can do and be anything.

Brainstorm a list of the things that make you happy. Maybe there's a favorite song that makes you happy, or maybe you have a favorite flower. When you find yourself slipping into a negative attitude, pick something from the list. Play your favorite song or find a bunch of your favorite flower. It's hard to be negative when you are happy.

Being positive is a perspective. It is a choice. When something negative or bad happens, always look for the silver lining to lift you out of the negative. And remember, these are our growth opportunities.

The next time something bad happens, find three positive things. They can even be ridiculous or silly. For example, maybe on the way to work, you got rear-ended and had a fender bender. Silver lining #1: You walked away and no one was seriously injured. Silver lining #2: You got out of a meeting you were dreading. Silver lining #3: The attendant at the auto-body repair shop asked you out, and you end up dating. Sometimes, there is Guardian Angel orchestration and coordination going on, even when the bad stuff happens.

LET GO OF THE OUTCOME

Our Guardian Angels are always there to help us, but it isn't always in the way we expect. When we release our judgment of the outcome, we free up our angels to do even more on our behalf. Let them have a greater plan, by not attaching a judgment or expectation to the outcome. When we release our expectation on the outcome, we also let go of the stress attached to it.

The next time you need to call on your Guardian Angel for help, do so without telling them how to help you. For example, maybe during your meditation, you tell your angel that you are stressed about an upcoming meeting that you are dreading. But stop there. Don't ask for them to handle it a certain way, just simply ask for them to help you find a way to be able to handle it. And then, when you get in a fender bender like the one in the previous scenario, thereby missing the meeting and having everything resolve without you having to be there, laugh, and say thanks.

SHARING OUR BURDENS

Remember that our Guardian Angels know us better than we know ourselves. When we let go of our judgment of the outcome, we reiterate our trust and faith in them. Our trust and faith in our Guardian Angels is the strongest link we have to them. When we release our burdens to our angels, and trust them to handle it, we also release some of the stress tied to the situation.

The next time you are worried about something, give it to your angels to handle. Imagine yourself placing your worries in a bag. Hand it to your Guardian Angel and simply say, "Help me with this." Watch as they take it up to their Angelic Realm. Notice how you feel, right now. Notice, how it feels like a weight has been lifted.

TAKING CARE OF OURSELVES

Living with good intentions is hard work. Recharging our bodies is important and necessary. We all can agree that there aren't enough hours in the day to accomplish everything that we want to get done, but there are a few simple things we can all make sure we are doing each day to take care of ourselves.

Eat good, healthy food. Allow yourself a treat every now and then. Don't always eat when you are on the run. Try to sit down for your meals whenever you can. Sitting down to eat makes us mindful of the moment. It is an acknowledgment that your mealtime is a few precious minutes to recharge.

Listen to your cravings, especially if they are healthy. If you are craving sugar, eat fruit. If you are craving greens, eat salad. When we tune into a higher frequency, our food cravings can actually be our body telling us exactly what it needs.

Drink enough water. We are in a day and age of fancy coffees, specialty drinks, craft beers, and excellent wine. But remember that everything is better in moderation. And don't forget to drink water, too.

Get enough sleep. When we are sleeping, our angels can connect with us. They have less time if we are up until all hours of the night. Not to mention, when we are rested, we are better able to deal with life's challenges. We have more patience, and it's easier to stay positive and hopeful when we've had a good night's sleep.

Stay balanced. We are all juggling a lot of different balls in the air at any given time. When we focus our attention too much on just one of them, the others fall. Figure out what you need to do to keep yourself balanced.

Treat yourself. Whether it's a warm Epsom salt bath, indulging in an episode of your favorite television program, or even just giving yourself an extra ten minutes to close your eyes, the result will be a release and a recharge of your energy.

Listen to your body. Don't ignore your own needs. When you are hungry, eat. When you need to work out to burn some energy, do it. If you are simply too tired to go for the run you planned to take, rest instead. By listening and taking care of our own bodies, we are respecting ourselves the way our Guardian Angels respect us.

GIVE YOURSELF A BREAK

Remember that our Guardian Angels love us unconditionally. They forgive us without judgment. Remember that we are here on this Earth to have a human experience. We will make mistakes. When we make mistakes, often, our biggest critic is ourselves. When we make mistakes, we need to forgive ourselves the same way our angels forgive us.

The next time you find yourself making a mistake, do whatever visualization exercise you need to do to let it go. Forgive yourself, and make a promise to yourself, "I will do better next time."

GIVE OTHERS A BREAK

By loving us unconditionally, our Guardian Angels are setting an example for us. By loving others unconditionally and without judgment, we reach a different level of love, and ultimately, a higher frequency. Accepting others unconditionally and without judgment is not easy. We are humans. We have a lot of opinions. Some of these opinions are wrapped up in what others should do and how they should behave and act. But remember, we can only control our own actions; we can't control what others do. We can't change people by our opinions, but we can encourage change by setting a good example. Everyone else is here to have a human experience, too; everyone will be making mistakes. Let that be their own business.

Try to break the habit of judgment. Start small. When you find yourself mentally criticizing someone else's clothing or personal food choices, stop. Grow into bigger examples. When you find yourself cursing someone else's actions, stop. For example, when a driver cuts you off, it's natural to be irritated. But let it go quickly and without judgment. The other driver didn't single you out personally. Sure, they should probably slow down and be more careful, but you can't make them do that. Remind yourself that you can only control your own actions, and you can choose not to escalate the situation.

Check your expectations at the door. Remember to love others for who they are, not what we expect them to be.

FIND YOUR PASSIONS

Nothing brings us more joy and happiness than when we are doing something we love and feel passionate about. Happiness and joy are natural connectors to the Angelic Realm. Fostering our passions gives honor and respect to a natural piece of ourselves. Pursuing our passions is uplifting and inspiring, to ourselves and others.

Make a list of the things you feel most passionate about. Are you dedicating enough time to your passions?

EMBRACE YOUR GIFTS

We all have different gifts and talents. The sooner we figure out what our strengths (and alternatively, weaknesses) are, we become closer to finding our purpose. Gifts are our natural talents and abilities, those things in life that come to us with ease or are naturally easy for us to do. Each and every one of us has different gifts that were given to us at birth.

Do you know what you are good at? Make a list of all of your talents and natural abilities. Those are your gifts.

When we combine our passions, with our gifts, amazing things can happen. We can begin to answer questions like, "Why am I here?" and "What am I suppose to do with my life?" When we take an inventory of our gifts and natural abilities and then go forth and look for work that uses those talents, our "job" becomes less of a job.

Think about if and how your gifts overlap with your passions. Is there anything you can do to bring your gifts and passions closer together?

An Angel Message

Find your personal strengths and the courage to complete the tasks at hand. Starting isn't easy, but finishing will be amazing.

THINK BEFORE YOU SPEAK

Our angels are extremely intelligent. But remember, they come from a different realm. Unlike our Spirit Guides, they have never walked on the Earth as human beings. They have a different frame of reference. Ask and you shall receive; however, we need to be careful how we ask. Words have a vibration and many words have several interpretations. Choose your words carefully. An example would be if our words are simply, "I need a break." If we step incorrectly off the curb and end up with a broken ankle, there is room to wonder if our Guardian Angel maybe incorrectly interpreted our words.

Be clear with your intention, so as not to leave room for misinterpretation. If you really need a break, send your request to your angel, complete with a visualization of what you mean.

LEARN THE LESSONS

We are all here on Earth, in this lifetime, to learn lessons. When our physical body dies, our souls return to Earth, time and again, to evolve and grow, and each time we are given lessons to help us achieve this goal. When we make mistakes, there is usually a lesson attached. When we cross paths with certain people, sometimes it is because we need to learn a lesson. By paying attention to these lessons and learning them, we can stop repeating them, over and over.

Think about recurring themes and lessons in your life. Maybe you are someone who is too "nice" to other people, and others have taken advantage of you, over and over. These types of people will keep coming into your life and this lesson will keep showing up for you until you learn it. The sooner we are able to recognize the pattern and learn the lesson, the quicker we can move past it.

FOLLOW YOUR HEART

Angels connect with us through our heart chakras. It's almost like we have heart strings connecting us to them. Our life is like a journey, and our heart is in the driver's seat. The open road is ours to explore, and there is no better navigational tool than your heart. Because we are connected to our Guardian Angels, every now and then they can give us a tug on our heart strings to pull us in the right direction.

We've already identified our passions and gifts. Chances are, you already know what your heart is calling you to do. Spend some time in meditation thinking about what your heart is calling you to do. Imagine a road map, and plot out some destinations that will help get you there.

When we face disappointment with anything directly connected to our heart's path it can feel amplified. We also need extra amounts of patience to wait for the opportunities, because when we are following our hearts, sometimes it feels like it is taking forever to get there. The result is that our hearts can end up feeling a little battered and bruised. When we are following our hearts, it is important to take extra special care of our hearts.

To take care of hearts, it can help to move with the flow. Know and trust that your Guardian Angel will be helping to align your journey with the right opportunities. We have to have the right amounts of dedication and hard work, but know that your Guardian Angel will line up the opportunities. Ask your Guardian Angel to help you not to miss them, or take a wrong turn.

When we face disappointment, it can be extra harsh. But disappointment and wrong turns are also a necessary part of the process. Overcoming disappointment is one of those life lessons we have to learn. When it happens, spend some time visualizing your heart. Imagine yourself going into a heart-shaped room. Visualize yourself cleaning up the cobwebs, and identifying all of the bruises and breaks. Hand them all over to your Guardian Angel by pointing them out. Now, bring in sparkles. Imagine these sparkles repairing all the breaks, sealing up the cracks, and bringing a fresh new energy to help keep your heart moving in the right direction.

FOLLOW YOUR GUT

Following our gut is different than following our heart. Our heart sets the course for the duration, our gut helps us to make the right turns and navigate the day-to-day decisions. When we have a choice between two different options, our life training has taught us to use our logical and rational thinking skills to make a choice. And yet, our logical brain is often influenced by preexisting thought patterns and belief systems—for example, the worry about what others will think, or who will be judging the outcome of our decision. But by now, we have also learned it is important to follow our "feeling" as well, and "feeling" isn't as easy to recognize; we have to tune into it. Now that we have learned to connect with our Guardian Angels, and understand that this "gut feeling" is coming through our solar plexus from them, we can better justify listening to it and utilizing it within our decision-making process. Trusting this feeling that comes from our Guardian Angels will never fail us.

The next time you are faced with a decision, use your logical brain first to come up with an answer. Next, check in with your intuition, your gut. Does that decision "feel" right? Or perhaps your angel is advising you not to worry about what anyone else thinks. Perhaps your angel is showing you a different option.

They say "hindsight is twenty-twenty." As you begin to implement a "gut check" into your decision-making process, pay attention to the outcome. When you followed your gut, what happened? Maybe something better than you originally expected?

BE YOUR TRUE SELF

By finding our passions, recognizing our gifts, following our heart and our gut, we are setting ourselves up perfectly to become our true, authentic selves. It is a lot of work to be someone you are not. It is a lot to work to hide our passions and true colors and live as anything but our own special, unique selves. When we bust out of our shells—when we live to our potential and when we live by our true colors—our biggest fans, the Guardian Angels, nearly explode in celebration.

Close your eyes and imagine yourself wrapped in an egg shell. This shell is made up of other people's expectations and judgment. It is made up of preexisting belief systems and old thought patterns. It is dark inside. Slowly, start tapping on the shell until you make a small hole. A beam of light shines in, and you can faintly hear your Guardian Angel cheering for you. Tap more and more, until you've made lots of holes, and the inside of the shell is filling up with light, and you can hear your angel's voice much more clearly. Now, punch and kick until the rest of the shell is laying in pieces around you. Look at yourself, as if you were seeing yourself for the first time. What do you see?

BE AN ORIGINAL LEADER

Every single person walking on this Earth is different than every other. Each one of us is unique, with our own complicated combinations of talents and gifts. We all have angels walking right next to us. Let that give us the faith and strength to be an original leader. Have the courage and confidence to be a trendsetter. Share with the world your brightness and originality, your passion and purpose. Lead by example, and lead by trusting that others have Guardian Angels in their driver seats, too.

 Close your eyes and imagine that your soul is a big ball of light. Your light shines so that others may be inspired by you and the example you set. Let your light keep shining, and grow it brighter and brighter. Imagine that your light is so strong, it can light the lights of others. Their lights grow stronger and stronger, until theirs is strong enough to light the lights of others. Now step back, and see all this light and love that started with you.

PERSEVERE

We have all begun challenges that turn out to be difficult to finish. We have all found ourselves facing unexpected challenges. In these times, our Guardian Angels call on us to persevere. Yet, they also remind us they are right there next to us to help us find the strength and courage we need in order to succeed.

 The next time you find yourself facing a challenge and you feel like giving up, imagine yourself running a long race, a marathon perhaps. You have reached the point where your body is feeling immense physical pain. Your muscles no longer seem to work. The doubt is creeping in and your brain is shouting, "I can't do this." And then, your Guardian Angel is there next to you. They take you by the hand and say, "Yes you can. You can do this." Let them pull you along. Let them take the pain away. Let them step in and help you. And then, imagine yourself crossing the finish line, triumphant.

CELEBRATE ACCOMPLISHMENTS

Our Guardian Angels call on us to celebrate. Our accomplishments serve as milestones and markers in our life. We need to recognize them. Recognizing our accomplishments also creates joyful memories. Our Guardian Angels get excited when we are excited. They are happy and joyful when we are happy and joyful. They understand and appreciate our achievements because they were right there with us throughout.

How do you like to celebrate? Sometimes, we throw parties. Other times, we may keep our celebrations more intimate. Whichever you choose, know that your Guardian Angel is right there with you.

GRATITUDE

When we start to realize the divine influence in our lives that comes to us through our Guardian Angels, it is difficult not to be thankful. We have been placed in exactly the right time and place to see the works of God. Acknowledging this divine source, and expressing gratitude and appreciation, we are simultaneously filled with love.

Never forget to say "thank you." It does not need to be elaborate, or fancy. As long as you express some whisper of gratitude that comes from you heart, your angels will hear it.

LOVE

Love is an energy that brings us together. We can love places, people, and even things. We learn unconditional love and acceptance from our divine, higher power and the Guardian Angels. There is no limit to unconditional love; it is bountiful and never-ending. Love is powerful, and it can last forever. It also has a built-in power of protection.

Think of someone you've lost. Maybe a parent or grandparent. Think of your love for them, a a great big ball of pink light. Think of them now as a soul in heaven and send them this ball of light, as if it were a balloon. It finds them in heaven, and encircles them, wrapping them in love. They, in turn, can send love in this same balloon-like ball of light, back to you.

Now send balloon lights of love out to all of your friends and family members. Imagine it dropping down on top of them, and surrounding them with unconditional love and acceptance. Add an extra layer of protection. Maybe you see someone, or hear about someone on the news who you know could use some extra love in their life. We can send these balloon lights to anyone, anywhere. Now, think about if the whole world was doing this for each other. Think about how the power of love can change the world.

BE NOT AFRAID

Fear is a language of awareness, a call to us to react or overcome. It is a phenomenal tool to warn us to react or heighten our awareness of a situation. But when we react to fear, it is often in a defensive manner, and often a fight-or-flight response. Make no mistake, fear is an unpleasant emotion. While fear can serve as a warning, fear can also cripple us. Our Guardian Angels want us to take a logical approach to fear, and not let it overcome our reasoning and logic. They also remind us that we have our own personal guardian, and the entire realm of angels can be at our side at any time, on a moment's notice; all we have to do is ask. Be not afraid, for they are with us.

The next time you find yourself feeling afraid, call your angel to your side and hand over your fear. Put it in a bag and give it to them to take and carry away for you. Set yourself in the middle of a bubble, clear out the negative, and fill it with positive light and love. Ask your angel to protect it and keep it safe.

LIVE WITHOUT REGRET

By becoming present with the angels, we come closer and closer to living a life without regret. By following our Guardian Angel's divine guidance, we learn to use our talents and gifts to pursue our passions. We learn the lessons our souls need to learn during this human experience. We follow their guidance to help others. We learn to love unconditionally, and accept love in return.

When you wake up each morning, make a promise to yourself that you will do the best you can with what you have. When you go to sleep at night, evaluate your day, claim your triumphs, and acknowledge your tribulations and mistakes. What could have gone better? What would you do differently? Recognize and celebrate when you get to the end of a day and realize, honestly, you did the best you could with what you had. By living each day without regret, we come closer to living a satisfied life here on Earth.

GO FORTH

When growing our intuition and awareness, we are growing into spirituality. While traveling this divine path as laid out by our Guardian Angels, we will come upon curves and turns. Sometimes, our path may feel uncomfortable or we will laugh at the strangeness we encounter, yet, this path will also be filled with enough amazing and incredible moments where we can't help but know we are on the right one. We can let that smile on our face become permanent. We can relax with faith and trust in ourselves and our angels.

An Angel Message

Your heart is unique and special.
It is filled with passion and purpose that is unique and special;
a complicated combination created just for you.
We will guide you on your path, encouraging you all the way to
release your fears and to touch the hearts of others
with kindness, compassion, and love.

PART FIVE

Extras and Milestones

ELEMENTS

Earth (Nature)

There is power in Nature. Spending time in nature can ground us and help us reestablish our roots to our human connection and experience. By grounding ourselves in nature, we remind ourselves that we are in the here and now of this lifetime. And yet, through nature, we can also reconnect with the divine. Nature has a way of reaching the crescendo of intensity that heightens our awareness.

Go outside and sit. Feel the sun and air on your skin. Smell whatever the breeze is bringing your way. Listen to the rustle of the trees or the sounds of the animals. Feel your feet beneath you connected to the Earth. Know that you are here, now, having and living a human experience with a divine purpose.

Fire

Fire brings us warmth and strength. It can be unpredictable if not contained. Let your fire burn within you, giving you strength to face whatever challenges life brings your way. Control your fire—use it for warmth and strength, but don't let it burn out of control.

Gather a group of friends and build a campfire. Smell the fresh air, and feel the warmth of the flames. Notice what happens around a fire: Stories are shared, and maybe even hopes and dreams are revealed. When sitting together, encircling a fire, there is a connection to yourself, others, and nature.

Water

Water is refreshing; it flows effortlessly. It takes many forms, from a stream to a river filled with rushing waterfalls, or a pond, lake, or ocean. There is magic that happens with water—from the creatures that can live below its surface, to the life source it provides to every living, breathing plant and animal.

The next time you have the chance, go and sit for a few minutes by a waterfall. Or if there isn't one nearby, imagine yourself sitting by one. Feel the tiny droplets of water that escape through its mist. Hear the thunderous crash as the water falls, pounding onto the rocks below. Recognize the endless flow and cycle.

The next time you have a chance to go for a swim, dive under the water. Feel the water on your skin and through your hair. Are you comfortable in and under water? Or do you find yourself feeling afraid? It's okay to be in awe of the power water can have. Embrace this awe, and know that your Guardian Angel is right there next to you, feeling what you feel.

Air/Sound of Silence

There is power in wind—so much so, that it can be harnessed to produce energy. Wind can carry sound, leaves, all sorts of things along with it. Wind can produce powerful storms and is sometimes an unpredictable force of nature.

 The next time there is a windy day, sit and listen and feel the breeze. What is it bringing you? What is it saying?

 Listen to the sounds of silence. It is a sound you can hear from the air, from the trees rustling in the wind, to the animals, bugs, and birds sending their music across the airwaves. This Zen moment can create a rhythm within your body as it comes into balance with nature, with your Guardian Angel right by your side.

WEATHER

Weather can be wild and unpredictable. It can be a source of worry in our lives. Perhaps there is a big outdoor event planned, and having good weather is critical. We can seek divine guidance in times like these.

 The next time you have to depend on the weather for an outdoor event, ask for guidance when picking the date. Look at the calendar and call in your Guardian Angel. Is there a day that stands out in your mind as better than the rest?

 As you approach a special event scheduled for outside, spend some quiet time thinking about it, on several different occasions. Ask your Guardian Angel for their help in making it a special day. Envision the weather, exactly as you would like to experience it. Place your trust in your Guardian Angel, and also ask them to open up an alternative option if the weather doesn't cooperate as you would like.

CHILDREN

Children have a special relationship with angels. Their connection is free and easy. They interact with angels all the time without even realizing it. As children get older, more and more doors to the angels shut, and the connection with them can become faint, as belief systems and barriers begin to lock into place. As adults, we can help encourage the children in our lives to keep these lines of communication open and not shut the doors.

If you have children in your life, share your personal experiences and interactions with your own Guardian Angels. Encourage them to talk about their own angels, and be open. Show them some signs that angels are in our lives, like keeping an eye out for feathers or heart shapes.

ANIMALS

Our pets teach us unconditional love and satisfy a human need for companionship. Their devotion to us, and ours to them, is a unique spiritual connection that is similar to our connection with our Guardian Angels. They bring us comfort and joy.

Have you ever understood what your pet needed when they needed it? They obviously can't tell you with words, but sometimes, we just know they need to go out, or we know when they are asking for a treat or want to play. Sometimes, it's because of their behavior. But consider that we are reading our pet's energy, and maybe it's more of a telepathic connection. Play with this. When you need to leave, sit with your dog or cat for a minute and look them in the eyes. In your head, imagine what time it will be when you get home. What will it look like outside? (For example, before or after dark?) Send this picture to your pet.

All animals are special, yet there are a few to mention here that carry special meaning.

Dolphins

Dolphins are angels of the sea. They swim with grace over, under, and through the waves. They bring a perfect harmony of movement and an extra level of gentleness to the Earth.

The next time you feel unsettled or out of sorts, imagine yourself swimming in the ocean with the dolphins. Follow them as they fly through the water. Let their rhythmic motion calm you from the inside out.

Bobcat

The bobcat's ears carry with it their own reminder from the angels. They have tufts of fur that poof out from their ears and look like an angel's wings. The animals in the cat family have their own special unique traits. Cats are patient and full of stealth, and they carry strength in leaps and bounds.

The next time you feel uncertain about a situation, think about a bobcat. Use your stealth to look at all sides of an issue. Be patient, and wait for the right answer to present itself. Know that you have the strength to carry it through.

Moose

The moose travels through the forest with strength and courage. Seeing one stops us in our tracks, filling us with awe and wonder. Their rack rises above; their steadfast stare captures our gaze. The bell of their bunchy neck provides extra protection from the dangers of the outdoors.

The next time you feel like you are lost and don't know which way to turn, imagine yourself standing in a forest. But then, a moose steps across your path. Follow it—grab on to their neck if you need to—and know that, like the moose, your angels will lead you through.

Wolf

The adventurous, strong wolf has pulled itself back from the brink of extinction. Loyal and strong, it howls at the moon and carries itself with ease and assurance. Its presence is intimidating, symbolic of predator and prey; it does its job to bring balance to the forest.

The next time you could use some extra strength and courage to face a situation, think about the wolf. Let it bring you the strength and courage you need to get through. Stand up tall, and carry yourself with grace just like the wolf. If you are on a righteous path, know that you, too, can be a catalyst for natural balance.

ARCHANGELS

Archangels are specialty angels, tasked with special areas of attention and concern. While our Guardian Angels are always with us, by our side, archangels can be anywhere and everywhere, helping anyone who calls upon them. When you are walking the divine path as instructed by your Guardian Angel, you also have access to these special teams.

Their light energy is so great and strong, they can send slivers of themselves anywhere, any time. They are moved by devotion and divine love.

Archangel Michael

Archangel Michael is the angel of strength, truth, courage, and protection. He watches over those who carry respect and humanitarian kindness.

Archangel Michael is an angel of honor, truth, and hope. When you feel "up against the world," Archangel Michael is a warrior angel and a good name to call upon when you feel threatened. Archangel Michael is rather easy, as well as delightful, to connect with.

The next time you find yourself feeling threatened or scared, don't hesitate to call Archangel Michael to your side. He can be anywhere, on a moment's notice, even if others have called on him for protection. His spirit is large, and multidimensional, and strong enough that he can be many places and with many different people, at the same time.

Find a fight song. We all have favorite songs that inspire us, some fill us with emotion or nostalgia, but there are also songs that give us hope and fill us with courage and determination. Find a song that fills you with courage and a desire to keep fighting. And listen to it whenever you need to call Archangel Michael to your side.

Archangel Gabriel

Archangel Gabriel offers wonderful support. He is especially there for us when we need to overcome a difficult chapter within our lives. He helps us by offering encouragement and motivates us to find and take the necessary steps to climb up and out of our situation. His hands offer great guidance and support.

When you find yourself feeling like you are struggling through an especially difficult time, imagine that you are standing on a staircase. This staircase is special, because it leads you up and out of your difficult situation. Imagine that Archangel Gabriel is standing on the step just above you. He reaches out, and takes your hand. One by one, he leads you up, step after step. You might not be able to see the end of the staircase yet, but with Archangel Gabriel's support, encouragement, and guidance, you soon will.

Archangel Raphael

Archangel Raphael is an archangel dedicated to offering extra support in the healing process. When we call upon Archangel Raphael, in addition to the healing power of our own Guardian Angel, he can also lend his power and support.

The next time you are in need of a big healing miracle, don't forget to call on Archangel Raphael. Imagine that he is standing next to you, and everything about his essence exuberates light, love, and healing. Imagine that this light extends out to you. It envelopes you in healing energy, washing through any and every bit of you that needs to be healed.

Calendar of Angels

Our angels have their own special calendar filled with ways to assist us. They love when they are able to fill new moments with tenderness and create sentimental memories. This calendar helps our angels oversee our vacation times. It also provides a tool for the angels to help turn an unexpected moment into a miracle. By being aware that such a calendar exists, we can tune our hearts into it. Know that our angels have a master calendar, and they are always working to fill it with light and protection.

The next time you are thinking about a vacation, take a few moments to check in with your angels. Maybe ask between two different destination options. Do you get a feeling that one might be better than the other? Or maybe you get a whisper of an answer. Next, look at your calendar and ask your angel about the dates you are thinking of going. Does your angel agree? Or maybe your attention is drawn to a different departure day, or maybe even a different week altogether.

MONTHS

January

January is the first month of our year's cycle: the month of "Janus" where every day in this month is of pure spirit, where cell doors are open for planning your future. It holds perfection and unlimited possibilities. As we thoughtfully reflect on our past events, we can give ourselves permission to achieve new and different potentials. It is a time to consider our passion and purpose.

Spend some of your meditation time during the month of January reflecting on the past year. What were your challenges? What were your achievements? Spend some concentrated time this month letting go of past hurt and upset, celebrating your accomplishments, and setting your intentions for the year ahead.

February

February is the shortest of all twelve months. It is a month of hibernation, or purification. Our pure spirit of "Februa" helps us to focus on building momentum by celebrating what we love from our youth and building it into our wisdom age. This delicate month is a time to stoke our passionate fire and shine our inner lights; the result will be a manifestation of your true beauty.

Sometime during the month of February, reflect on some of your favorite memories as a child.

Sometime during the month of February, evaluate your passions. Are you pursuing them enough? Is there anything you need to make time for in the year ahead?

This is the month where every four years we get an extra day. By taking a "leap," we can encourage the growth of new goals and motivation. Take advantage of this extra day, think of it as a gift and use it to take a "leap." This extra day possesses the power to unleash a huge breakthrough in our lives. Take a leap of faith. Your Guardian Angels will be there waiting to help you fly and to catch you if you should fall.

Imagine yourself standing on the edge of a cliff. On the other side of the cliff is something that you really want to go for. Close your eyes and leap towards it, and imagine your Guardian Angel is giving you a boost, and helps you land safely and securely on the other side.

March

March is a month of thirty-one days. It is a month of hard work and when the year's journey really begins. In March, we close the door to the winter's darkness, and open the screen door to the fragrance and rebirth of spring. It is a month of wonder and change. While the month is often unpredictable, it's hard not to feel enlightened and nurtured. Seeds are being planted, and dreams begin to take on a life of their own. The work in the garden begins, and we are reminded that all is well when we see the red-crested robins go flying by.

March is an important month to have a strong connection to faith. During the month of March, focus on strengthening your connection with your Guardian Angel.

During the unpredictable month of March, march forward, walk with a pep in your step, and keep a steady pace. Doing so will help to keep you in balance. It is an important month to practice self-care, as you work through the changes and transitions the month will surely bring.

April

In the full swing and spirit of spring, April is a month of settling in. The unpredictable month of March has passed, and the warmth and beauty of the month of April arrives, reassuring us that all is right with the world. The fragrances are fresh, and new birth surrounds us. The warmth of the sun is on our skin and we remember that life is good.

During this month of rebirth, spend time out in nature. Use all of your senses to see, smell, feel, hear, and know that all is right with the world. Take in its beauty; be grateful for the physical signs that after the darkness, comes light.

May

May is a month of inner knowing. The beautiful feminine expression of "knowing" is awakened in a rather large and deep desire to show the world an inner light. It is an expression of a purpose. It is a time to tune into your higher awareness and just dance. May is an expressive month, and it is a time to bloom to the fullest heights. The month of May also has a way to blend the calmness of nature and beauty with your home and sacred spaces.

Sometime during this month, find a set of garden charms or wind chimes and place them in your yard or garden. Place an array of quartz crystals near them, and this will amplify the energy of your garden. It will make coming home feel wonderful.

Whenever possible during the month of May, bring the outside in. Cut flowers from your garden and place them on the table. Open your windows. A fresh breeze and the fragrance of the flowers drifting in through the window will feel as if the angels personally came in and blessed everything.

The month of May is not a time to hide talents, passions, and dreams. Dance if you feel like dancing; sing if you feel like singing. Let your light shine, and be yourself.

June

June is a month of sunshine. June stimulates extreme perception and sensitivity. From light, sound, and touch, the feeling of being connected to the divine is significant. June is the center of the year and the time to focus on the center of our spiritual soul. It is the pivotal point of growth, to make sure you are pacing yourself and staying focused.

June is a month where it is easy to get distracted. Make sure to balance play time and the first fun weekends of summer with your soul's passion and purpose.

An Angel Message

Keep a sunny disposition in your heart, and the angels will marvel with a love that is intoxicating. They will enhance your confidence in all that needs to be manifested through the power of your inner light.

July

July gives us thirty-one days filled with shifts of change. The vibration of the month of July sends messages of transition that can carry our determination to a higher level that is more refined. July is filled with reasons to celebrate our independence, our freedom, and our human experience here on Earth. Our creative mighty angels add color to our life and help light up July.

This is a month to tune in to color and brilliance. Observe the colors of summer everywhere around you. Observe the colors in the sky lit up by fireworks. Let these colors inspire you and fill you with awe.

An Angel Message

The month of July carries persistence and determination, yet sets the limits as the light spirit is becoming more refined.

August

The month of August is filled with desires and a willingness to reach a higher level. This month will provide solitude specifically to give us a chance to appreciate all that we have worked for, the opportunities that have been provided, and all of the areas in which we have prospered. Taking advantage of this moment of solitude will open us to enlightenment and bring with it positive energy. It will also bring courage to accept our importance in the world.

Find a quiet moment some time this month. Perhaps it is a quiet morning in the garden, sitting with a cup of coffee. Or maybe there is a quiet night where you can sit on the porch and listen to the sounds of late summer— crickets chirping and locusts singing. Take a few moments to think about how far you've come, and appreciate the opportunities that have come your way. Let yourself fill with courage and determination to keep going, and know that more good things are just around the corner.

September

The month of September brings with it another change of season. This is an ideal time to create a new design for ourselves. September is not an average month by any means; it brings with it a range of highs and lows, warms and colds. It is a time to take our divine willpower, and balance our mind, body, and spirit together as we grasp a fresh new look.

As you shift from a summer schedule of outdoor activities, and what is often a more relaxed pace, let yourself be rejuvenated by this change. Embrace new tasks and projects, and let yourself be inspired by the change.

October

October is the tenth month of the year, and we start winding down to the finish. It is a time to celebrate how far we've come, and yet still hold everything in balance knowing the end is in sight. Stay on track, just a little longer. We can let ourselves begin to celebrate how well we held it together during unexpected changes. We can feel a strength in knowing that our Guardian Angels will be there, encouraging us foe rest of the way.

Think about the last few miles of a marathon. Think about how far the runners have come, and think about all of those who line up to cheer them the last few miles. When a runner reaches the very last mile, that mile will often take care of itself. It's the last two miles before that when a runner needs to hear the loudest cheers. Know that our angels are cheering us on, especially during this month. The last two months will take care of themselves, so you just need to take care of this one.

November

November is a month of strength that can ensure progress and achievement. By being our genuine creative self and having strength in our convictions, we will easily attract others. By knowing our soul's mission, and staying pure in our purpose, we line ourselves up for success in our journey. If we take advantage of this strong month and work hard, we can position ourselves to make great strides along our path.

This is a good month to dedicate yourself to something in line with your passion and purpose. Make a commitment this month to accomplishing something towards this, and know that you will move towards your goals further within this month, more than any other.

December

December is a time to go deep within ourselves to prepare for a shift into new endeavours. A month of shadows, we can follow the light within the month of December to gather together all of the last twelve months of experiences to find the new wisdom we gained. A month of darkness and hibernation, our Guardian Angels can be the lights of hope and peace that continue shining through. December is a time to have a cosmic awareness that there is something greater, and we can let ourselves be inspired by this awareness.

December has the darkest days of the entire year. Throughout this month, look for and notice the lights. Look for the holiday lights on houses and trees; count the candles in windows and on dining room tables. Notice how these lights shine through the darkness, bringing a sense of peace and feelings of hope. Remember that no matter how dark it gets, there will always be a light to find.

DAYS OF THE WEEK

Our souls follow a cycle of energy from day to day as the week goes on. By keeping a few ideas in mind from one day to the next, we can help ourselves progress, week by week.

Monday / Moon

Monday is the beginning of the moon week. When we go into the week with awareness that there will be unpredictable energies, and there will be new challenges to face, we open up a new flow of energy within ourselves that will help us navigate these unpredictable energies. Monday is a day where we feel recharged and renewed and ready to deliver.

Monday morning has arrived. Before you place your feet on the floor on Monday morning, this is a good time of the week to check in with your angel to ask what the week ahead has in store for you. By checking in before we get lost in our morning routine, we will be more likely to find a sense of joy and look forward to the new week.

Tuesday / Mars

Tuesday is a day for honesty. Tuesday is a day to be true to our own selves, and be thoughtful about our present strategies. Tuesday is a day where we've gotten into our week, but not too far. It is still possible to change course, if a directional change is needed.

Tuesday is a good day to check course and be honest with yourself. On Tuesday, ask yourself if you are on track. Check in with your activity level and focus. Has your week started off in the way that you wanted? If the answer is no, there is still plenty of time to change direction and try something different.

Wednesday / Mercury

Wednesday is the day that opens up to the heavens. It can be a day of divine communication, where our soul can more easily connect to receive a download of new ideas. Wednesday is a day to be aware of synchronicities and serendipity in socializing and communication.

Wednesday is a good day to pay attention to your lines of communication with both your Guardian Angel and others. Do you have any new ideas that might have popped up? If so, write them down; they are probably important. Are you finding communication with some easier than others? If so, these are important connections. Are there people who you have completely failed to connect with today? If so, maybe that's a divine sign that this person isn't the one you need for that task or issue.

Thursday / Jupiter

Thursday is a day to be aware of all that we need to balance. On Thursday we have the task of balancing the positive with the negative. As we grow in awareness and knowledge regarding our spiritual growth, we tune into the pressures and responsibilities that come with it. But Thursday is a day where balance can manifest in wealth, in the law of attraction, wherever we need. Because of this, Thursday is a good day to be aware of all your hopes and dreams.

Spend some quiet time thinking about all of the different things you balance in your life. Do any feel off kilter or out of balance? Thursday is a good day to focus on realigning anything that might be out of balance. Identify any balance issues, and ask for guidance to get back into balance.

Imagine that your body is like a car, and schedule a tune-up with your Guardian Angel. Ask for a scan to determine any physical imbalances. Are there any adjustments you need to make sure your body is physically balanced?

Friday / Venus

Friday is a day of love. It is naturally a day of looking back and forward at the same time; we look back on a week of trouble and triumphs and look forward to the weekend ahead. Friday is a day where we can find comfort in looking back to see how far we've come and a day where we can find comfort in looking forward, with the knowledge that we are putting our energy into our passion. Friday is a day of indulging and celebration.

On Friday, look back and review your week. What were your troubles and challenges from the week? What were your triumphs and accomplishments? Learn from your mistakes and challenges, and release them into the universe. Celebrate your achievements and look forward to the weekend ahead.

Saturday / Saturn

Saturday is a significant day in the weekly cycle because it is a catchup day. It is an opportune time to count your harvest and a great day to organize and meditate. It is a day to find time for ourselves and take care of our needs.

Weekends are busy times. It is easy to get lost in doing tasks around the house and helping others. Every Saturday, pick at least one activity to do for yourself. Whether it's going for a walk or visiting with a friend, pick an activity that energizes you and do it.

Saturday is a good day to let the old inspire the new. Find something in your life you would like to change. Examine the old way of doing it, and let that inspire the change and the new way.

Sunday / Sun

Sunday is a day of rest and play. It is a day to rejuvenate and have a bit of fun. Doing so, will bring about clarity and a sense of well-being. A natural need for humans is a sense of safety and security. By taking time to stop and rest, we reenergize ourselves and can find clarity. This in turn, will amplify our sense of safety and security in our world, and how we navigate through it.

Find one restful thing to do every Sunday. It can be as simple as designating Sunday as the one day you don't use an alarm to wake up.

Find one playful thing to do every Sunday. It doesn't have to be the same thing each Sunday, just one thing that brings you joy and makes you feel like you are having fun.

SEASONS

Winter

Winter is a season to notice contrasts: light within the dark, warmth within the cold. The silence in winter is like no other silence throughout the rest of the year. Yet, winter is a time of hibernation, where our spirit is growing, and changing, and being replenished.

Choose a day during the winter and go outside. Listen to the quiet. Observe the stillness of the air, the sounds of silence. Yet, think about everything that is sleeping and growing. The seeds nestled under the earth, the animals tucked away to stay warm and sleep. Know and understand that our spirit goes through these cycles too, growing and changing.

Spring

A boost from mother nature brings us a significant gift: new growth. The energy of spring can lift us up to embrace the new surprises of color and sweetness in our lives. Spring encourages us to "hurry up" and get a start on our new paths and to keep learning, seeing, and discovering all that we can in the time that we have.

 Take some time during this season to reflect on all of the ways you've grown since last spring. By acknowledging how far you've come, let it fill you with excitement for what might be coming next.

Summer

Summer is a time to stretch out our arms, feel the sun and air on our skin, and take a break. We can stop and appreciate all of the hard work we've done, and take a minute to soak up the radiant sunshine and goodness that summer life offers. More than any other time of year, summer offers us opportunities to relax.

 Summer can be a busy time of coming and going, taking advantage of the good weather to be outside, and participating in lots of activities. During the months of summer, remember to take time to relax, even if you have to plan it. Save a few summer days on your calendar to be "do nothing days." Let those days take you wherever you want to go and feel like doing on that day. On those days, if you feel like sitting in your garden and reading a book, do that. If you feel like going to the beach and taking a nap in the sunshine, do that.

Autumn

More than any other season, this is the month where we can see sudden shifts. The air can change from warm to cool, practically overnight. The leaves reflect this change in their brilliant colors and eventual fall from their tree. It is a time to harvest the summer growth.

 During the season of autumn, practice embracing change. Instead of being sad about saying goodbye to the swimsuits, be grateful for a warm cozy sweater and a hot apple pie. Look forward to crackling fires in the fireplace and the upcoming holiday season.

HOLIDAYS

New Year's

The New Year's holiday has such an air of celebration about it. It is a day to celebrate the achievements and accomplishments from the past year and let go of any disappointments. It is a time to look forward by making new promises. It is a day to let the old be in the past, and embrace the new year that has arrived.

As we usher out the old and welcome in the new, don't forget to hold a space for your Guardian Angel. Remember that they might have plans for you, too, and those plans might be different—and even better—than your own.

At every end, there is a new beginning. Take a moment to recap the events that have unfolded in the last year. Our Guardian Angels love when we acknowledge our memories. After you acknowledge and honor your triumphs and let go of your challenges and tribulations, get ready to slowly step into this new year. Thank your angel for standing by your side.

Valentine's Day

In a traditional sense, Valentine's Day is about pursuing and celebrating love. We engage in romantic acts big and small, from leaving a simple note to tell someone "I care" to planning an elaborate date night out with someone special. Valentine's Day is a day to feed your heart and acknowledge unconditional love. The center of our heart is, at the same time, sensitive and powerful.

Make a promise to yourself on Valentine's Day to let the kindness and compassion and love and acceptance that you feel in your heart on this day carry over into other days as well.

Easter

Easter is a celebration of the goodness of spring. Filled with symbolism, like eggs in baskets and bunnies and birds, the significance of the Easter holiday means many different things to many different people. But the joy in rebirth after a darkness, whether that be the Lenten season, or simply the darkness of winter, means it is a time to rejoice. Personally, my favorite symbol of Easter are the lilies. The whitest of lilies should grace every table of each and every home. A delicate and soft flower, the pure white lily represents the soul and hope for everlasting life.

Choose your own favorite symbol from the Easter holiday and traditions. Maybe it's the sweetness of special candies, or the celebration of color as represented in the Easter egg. Figure out and acknowledge why it is your favorite symbol, what about your symbol makes it so special for you? Taking a minute to figure out why something is special and holds meaning for you helps us in our connection to the Devine Realm of the angels.

Fourth of July

There is no other holiday that screams color in the way that the Fourth of July explodes with sparkle and excitement. A celebration of freedom and summer, the Fourth of July is a favorite of many. Unlike any other holiday, this holiday shouts to us to stop and observe all that is going on around us.

From the moment you get out of bed in the morning, use all of your senses to take in the day. Try to stop and notice everything going on around you throughout the day. It is usually a busy day, so this has the potential to be a challenging task. Enjoy the feel of the warm sun on your skin. Take in the smell of hamburgers on the barbecue grill. Listen to the crackle and snap of the campfire and admire the explosion of colors and beauty in a fireworks display.

Halloween

Halloween has its roots in the pagan holiday to celebrate the dead. The next day, November 1, is the religious holiday, All Saints Day. But traditionally, the night of Halloween is about making the scary, fun. It is about taking the fear out of what we would otherwise be frightened by. Halloween is about facing fears, and it's a day set aside to do just that.

On this day of facing fears, purge yours. Sit down and make a list. What are you afraid of? Pick one thing on the list, maybe it's the easiest, and make it your goal to face that fear. For example, if you are afraid of heights, give yourself a goal of going on a hike or taking a tour of a tall building. There is nothing more liberating, than to face—and conquer—something we fear.

Thanksgiving

A holiday of abundance, and sometimes even overindulgence, Thanksgiving is obviously a time to celebrate and be thankful for the many blessings in our lives. It is also a good reminder not to overdo it. That feeling in our belly, the one that tells us to stop eating because we are full, often gets ignored on a day like Thanksgiving.

Today, make sure to listen to your gut. Literally. Stop eating if you are full. Make today about the concept of "just enough." Eat just enough food to have what you want, without making yourself sick. Drink just enough wine so you don't overdo it. Practice the art of "just enough."

Christmas

Different religions celebrate different ideas during the holiday season, but any way you look at it, this holiday is about finding hope in the darkness. We celebrate each other by giving gifts, and we marvel at the wonder and magic in this holiday especially.

During this holiday season, look for and celebrate the magic in your life. What are some things in your life that feel magical? What are some of the reminders at the holiday season that take you back to the best memories of your childhood? Our angels love to be a part of our memories.

Birthdays

Each one of us gets our own special day each year. Our angels are there with us, waiting to celebrate our day. Sometimes, people hesitate to celebrate their birthday. However, this is our one special day, just for us, each year. This day has your name on it and carries a special imprint just for you.

Celebrate your birthday. It can be a quiet celebration, or a big birthday bash. The important thing is to honor your day in some special way. Your angel has a special gift just for you. On this special day, your special birthday wish carries a lot of extra strength in the Angelic Realm. Don't forget to make a wish.

LIFE MOMENTS

Birth

The day you take your first breath is a very special day. To be there when a new baby is welcomed into the world is just as special. A lot has been accomplished by the time this moment of new life arrives. A map of earthly endeavors has already been planned out. It includes lots of proud moments and accomplishments and some difficulties to overcome. This is also the moment of arrival for our Guardian Angels. They are assigned to us in the Divine Realm, and join us at birth. There truly is a miracle at birth.

The next time you hear about a new baby being born, pause for a moment. Think about how that baby also comes with a special angel. Take just a few moments and wish them well on their journey together.

Finding out about a Pregnancy

It is a special moment when a woman realizes she is pregnant. Sometimes, that moment is filled with pure joy; a dream is coming true. Other times, it comes as an unexpected shock, because sometimes it wasn't part of "the plan."

When you read that positive sign on the pregnancy test, it is bound to come with a lot of emotion. Whichever emotions those happen to be, stop and meditate. If you are looking for answers, know that they will come. If you are looking for meaning, trust that you will find it. Whatever you think or feel about the situation, know that it absolutely is part of the plan. It just might not have been one you knew about yet.

New Baby

A new baby is filled with pure innocence and hidden potential. But they need everything. Bringing a new baby home can be overwhelming, as this new little body requires all of your time and attention to be nurtured and taken care of. While it is a joyful time, it can also be a time of heightened insecurity. Everything is new, and it's hard to always know what to do. There are lots of people who want to offer advice, and there is probably a stack of how-to books somewhere nearby.

When you find yourself feeling overwhelmed, remember that your intuition can lead you to the answers. Also remember that there is a whole team of helpers working behind the scenes. This baby came to you by divine match. You were meant to be this child's parent. You already know this baby better than anyone else. Set aside the advice from well-meaning helpers and thoroughly written books, and let the baby tell you what he or she needs. Hold the baby in your arms, and imagine your angel talking to the baby's angel. Make an arrangement that all of you will work together to do the best you can for this new little person.

Illness in a Child

Part of having a human experience includes getting sick. It is hard enough when we get sick ourselves; it can be an especially helpless feeling to watch a child deal with an illness. But children naturally know about their angels. They are already operating at a high frequency filled with pure love from the angels. God blesses children with extra love; they trust their own imaginations. When a child gets sick, this is a natural opportunity to talk to them about their angels and help them grow in their faith.

When a child becomes sick or injured, talk to them about how their angel is always standing by their side, ready to help. Explain that their angel is filled with healing energy, and ask them to call on their own angel to help them get better. Have them imagine this healing energy extending from their angel, and going to the parts in their body that are sick or injured. Empowering children to help with their own healing will help them heal much faster.

Sometimes children need help clearing their chakras, too. If the child is old enough, choose one of the earlier chakra clearing exercises, and adapt it as necessary for a child. For really little ones, it can help to rub their tummies. Place your hand gently on the baby's tummy, rubbing in a clockwise motion. Call upon your Guardian Angel to helping the irritating illness of the child to melt away. This gentle motion can reopen their chakras and release the imbalance or the emotion that they may be holding inside of them.

Loss of a Child

Babies and children are deeply loved, both in heaven and on Earth. When a child dies, there are as many angels available as are necessary to help hold our emotions. There is no map for navigating the grief, depression, fatigue, exhaustion, and stress that comes with the loss of a child. Angels are there for you if you want them. Know that our littlest ones were already close to the heavenly realm when they were here in the earthly realm. Because their visit here was brief, it is easy for them to go back to heaven. Know that you can always talk to them out loud, and they will hear you and know you.

Take the time to pause and feel and grieve. Yet also take the time to step out of the sadness and to heal. Always remember, you are not alone. Nothing will help you know this more than to talk to your child out loud. They can always hear you. They know your sadness, they will try to bring you comfort when they hear your voice.

Loved One at War

In this day and age, some of our loved ones go off to serve and protect. Whether that be with the local police force or as a soldier in the military, it is helpful to know that there are warrior angels. We can call on them to keep our soldiers safe. We can ask that they please stand by and carry our loved ones serving safely home. Sending prayers across the world creates a prayer chain. The intention is typically a silent vibration of an individual prayer that collects momentum as it travels through the universe. This vibration finds its way to the ones who need it the most.

When a loved one goes off to war, whether it be your loved one or the loved one of someone unknown, send a prayer along with them. It doesn't have to be an official "prayer" per se, just a thought of good intention that the person stays safe and returns home.

ROMANCE

The angels of the golden hearts are with us when it comes to romance. Filled with compassion and ecstasy, they revel in the expression of love we have for ourselves and others. When love finds us, it comes with a certain vulnerability. It isn't always easy to open ourselves up to this vulnerability. Over the years, the hurt can build up and we lose faith and trust in others; it can be difficult to love. The angels with golden hearts are there to help protect our hearts.

 Think about how a child loves. They love freely and with reckless abandon. They love everything from the pony on the carrousel to the new friend they just met at the park. Take some time to imagine yourself loving freely and without worry in the same way a child loves. How would your life be different if you let go of past hurts and let yourself love and be loved?

 Does your heart need healing from a past hurt? The angels with golden hearts can help. Imagine these specialty angels, shrinking themselves down to the size of a small army. There is exactly the right number of these angels, as many as you need. They are going to work together to fix your heart. Imagine them encircling your heart center. They examine the cracks and know exactly how to fix the breaks. They repair what needs repairing. Next, they wrap your heart center with protection, giving it extra strength. Your heart is now almost ready to love again.

 Let go of past hurts. We all experience hurt and loss in our lives; it is part of having a human experience on Earth. But it is important not to carry past hurts into new relationships. Your new love interest is not the same person as someone who might have caused you hurt in the past. Don't hold the new person responsible for someone else's past wrongs. The best way to move forward with a new relationship is to forgive and release. Imagine yourself having a conversation with someone who has hurt you in the past. If this is scary or intimidating for you, call the angels with golden hearts to your side to help you. Also know that your own Guardian Angel is standing by your side. Tell this other person that you forgive them. This might take some time, but know that it is important if you want to move forward. Thank them for the lessons you learned because of them and the wisdom that hindsight has brought you. Next, imagine this person being wrapped in love from their own Guardian Angel. This love encircles them, and is ready to carry this person away to the next part of their own journey. Watch them go, and wish them well.

Marriage

Marriage is a fusion of two separate lives coming together. Romance and trust build into a distinct and special knowing. Providing emotional, physical, and spiritual support for one another is all signed onto a paper that is legally binding, "until death do us part." The bond together grows as shared experiences build, one on top of the other. Communication, honesty, trust, and respect are just a few of the tools needed to build this life together. Marriage is hard, yet rewarding work.

No one will ever teach us more about ourselves than our spouse. Cooperating with someone else to build a life together is not easy. We learn compromise, we learn our strengths, and we come to know our weaknesses, all because of daily interactions with this person we've chosen for ourselves. Be aware of and learn the lessons. Failure to learn the lessons will result in repeating patterns, and those habits will be harder to break the longer they are allowed to repeat. Our angels are always there for us, to help us understand and guide us through these life lessons.

Accept your partner for who they are, not what you expect them to be. Always remember that the only person we can truly change is ourselves. We can't control anyone else; we can only control how we handle ourselves. Remember to call on your Guardian Angel for their guidance and support.

Embrace spontaneity in your marriage. When we are together with the same person, it is easy to settle into comfortable routines. Yet changing things up every now and then will help to spark creativity and passion, and bring back some of those qualities that caused us to fall in love in the first place. Remember that your Guardian Angel is always there to offer suggestions and present opportunities whenever being spontaneous feels like a challenge.

Divorce

We are here on Earth to have a human experience; we are not expected to be perfect. We are here to learn the lessons we need to learn, and sometimes that means going through a marriage that ends in divorce. Carrying emotions like anger, regret, and fear inhibit growth and can weigh us down.

When a marriage ends, it is important to take time to grieve and process the experience. Let yourself feel all of the emotions you need to feel in order to get through this difficult time. But be careful not to let your emotions dictate your actions. Remember your Guardian Angel is always there with you, feeling everything you feel. They can help you process your emotions by holding them on your behalf while you figure out how to move forward.

Aging

Our bodies may age in the conventional way, but our hearts can stay young as long as we want them to. We can't control how our bodies age, but we can control our attitude. No one can take that attitude away from us. Our angels are right there with us, ready to help us stay young at heart.

 Stay true to your colors. By being our authentic selves, we naturally stay young at heart. Follow your passions and dreams, and you are well on your way to staying young at heart.

 Step outside of your comfort zone. Our Guardian Angels love when we challenge ourselves, and challenging ourselves naturally keeps us young at heart. Always challenge yourself to try new things, and experience everything that life has to offer.

An Angel Message

Invite adventure. And together we will create memorable and joyful moments together.

CONCLUSION

In hindsight, when you look back on your life, you may see how your journey may have placed you in the right moment of time to see or believe in miracles. As you look forward to your life's plan, remember to embrace your remarkable inner wisdom. These messages and these words quietly spoken to you, are for you to use. Angels in Heaven and on Earth are profoundly happy and appreciate when you slow down and trust in your intuition, for that is your Guardian Angel's voice within you.

Here is one last exercise for you.

Think about how you found this book. Did it call your name from a shelf? Did someone gift it to you and say, "You need to read this." Whatever the case may be, know that, without a doubt, finding this book was a gift from your Guardian Angel. Embracing this book and the concepts and techniques set forth within its pages is your gift back to your Guardian Angel.

An Angel Message

*My Beloved Child, you are certain that you know what is best for you.
Please trust that I speak through you. I feel what you feel,
I love what you love, I see what you see. Trust in me.*

*I know that you are stronger than you think you are.
You are more colorful than you express and you are sensory receptive
in many more ways than just one.*

*You are blessed with two realities—your thought
and your thinking. I am in your thoughts.*

—Your Guardian Angel

Annette Bruchu discovered the metaphysical world at an early age. But it wasn't until later in life that she realized she was not alone. Annette is a nationally known Intuitive Healer. She has a vast understanding of the auric fields, color representation, and chakra systems. She has the ability to naturally channel healing to all types of physical and psychic confrontations and teaches several intuitive development and energy healing courses. As a teacher and mentor, Annette seeks to empower others to develop their own intuitive and psychic gifts. Annette has been recognized by TopRecommendedProfessional.com as a top professional in holistic alternative energy work. Find her on Facebook at: www.facebook.com/helpingyouhealcenter.